Federalism and the Poor:

A Review of the Canada Assistance Plan

Policy
Study
Series

Ontario
Economic
Council

Derek P. J. Hum

© 1983
Ontario Economic Council
81 Wellesley Street East
Toronto, Ontario
M4Y 1H6

Printed in Canada

Canadian Cataloguing in Publication Data

Hum, Derek, 1944–
    Federalism and the poor

(Policy study series / Ontario Economic Council,
ISSN 0227-0005)

Bibliography: p.
ISBN 0-7734-8165-5

1. Canada Assistance Plan. 2. Federal-provincial
relations (Canada) I. Ontario Economic Council.
II. Title. III. Series: Policy study series (Ontario
Economic Council)

HV105.H8   362.5′82′0971   83-093021-3

This report reflects the views of the author and not necessarily those of the
Ontario Economic Council. The Council establishes policy questions to be
investigated and commissions research projects, but it does not influence the
conclusions or recommendations of authors. The decision to sponsor publication of this study was based on its competence and relevance to public policy
and was made with the advice of anonymous referees expert in the area.

To Jason and Justine

Contents

vi Contents

Tables

Figures

Acknowledgments

I would like to express my appreciation to the Ontario Economic Council for providing me with the opportunity to write this study. The Council's patience and support have been unstinting. The support of the Social Science and Humanities Research Council of Canada is also acknowledged. My debt to individuals is substantial. Gayle Oyama provided bibliographic assistance, Don Sabourin designed the necessary computer programs, and Frank Strain offered helpful comments at all stages of the study. Many individuals provided useful criticism of earlier drafts; I must especially thank David Conklin, James Dean, Joe Ryant, Enid Slack, and Paul Thomas, as well as anonymous reviewers. Special thanks must also go to Alex Scala for his patient and careful editing. None of the above are responsible for any errors that remain; nor are they necessarily sympathetic to the views expressed, which are those of the author alone.

FEDERALISM AND THE POOR: A REVIEW OF THE CANADA ASSISTANCE PLAN

1
Introduction

At the time of Confederation, the provision of assistance to the poor was a private and a local matter. Family, church, and voluntary charities were expected to provide support when necessary, and municipal governments stepped in only as a last resort. The British North America Act entrenched the localized provision of assistance by making it a provincial responsibility (but one that the provinces could freely leave to their municipalities). Yet it assigned the most significant sources of revenue not to the provinces but to the national government – an arrangement that implicitly acknowledged the prevailing conviction that social assistance was not, in normal circumstances, a responsibility of government at all.

This separation of resources and responsibilities did not at first create any serious difficulties. But with industrialization and a growing urban labour force came demands that strained the resources of private agencies and municipalities. Under pressure from the labour movement, Ontario became the first province to enter the field of social security, introducing a workmen's compensation scheme in 1914. Following the First World War, several provinces introduced mothers' allowances for widows with dependent children. It was in this period that the implications of the BNA provisions began to make themselves felt. Provincial governments had the formal power to undertake ambitious social programs, but not the resources. The federal government had the resources, but not the power.

Short of changing the Constitution, the only solution that offered itself was cost-sharing, an arrangement that provided the provinces with the wherewithal to undertake major programming and at the same time gave the federal government a measure of influence over social policy. Significant federal involvement in social security began with the passage of the Old Age Pensions Act in 1927.

Each province was expected to initiate and establish its own pension scheme, but provided certain stipulated conditions were met the federal government would cover 50 per cent of incurred costs. Since 1927 there have been many cost-sharing programs. One important arrangement is the Canada Assistance Plan (CAP), introduced in 1966 in order to provide a flexible and expanded system of federal grants for cost-shared social assistance programs (welfare) and social services (other than health and education[1]).

CAP was expected to achieve a number of aims: better and more comprehensive coverage for those in need of assistance, including the working poor; increased opportunities for the unemployed through vocational rehabilitation and upgrading of skills; and consolidation of assistance programs. In view of this ambitious program, the Plan was hailed by many observers as a landmark development in the history of Canada's social security system. Moreover, the negotiation of CAP was seen as a striking instance of successful federal-provincial cooperation. Consultations between Canada and the provinces had been frequent and sincere, agreement on major issues swift. In comparison with other federal-provincial negotiations, such as those related to the Canada Pension Plan, medicare, funding for education, constitutional review, and tax-sharing, 'the development of the Canada Assistance Plan was undoubtedly the most harmonious major product of federal-provincial relations in the 1960s' (Dyck 1976, 601–602). Yet by the early 1970s, it was clear that CAP had failed to live up to the expectations of its sponsors. This failure was due in part to provincial reluctance to follow the intent of the CAP legislation and in part to the inherent limitations of the legislation itself.

The most important portion of the CAP legislation had to do with general assistance and social services. Its wording put a clear emphasis on needs-testing. Earlier programs had been categorical, basing eligibility for assistance on membership in a designated group (the elderly, the blind, etc.). CAP required only that a recipient be 'in need or likelihood of need'. Therefore any individual judged in need on the basis of a provincially designed needs-test, whether employed or not, was potentially eligible for cost-shared assistance.

The move to de-categorize assistance programs through the introduction of a general needs-test was viewed as a major and novel policy direction. However, the federal government could only establish general guidelines; it could specify neither the precise conditions under which people would be eligible for income assistance nor the level of benefits. Because these matters have been left to the discretion of the provinces, the nature and scope of assistance programs varies

---

1 Health and education are also cost-shared and consolidated under the Established Programs Financing Act.

widely across Canada, and very little in the way of national standards of assistance have emerged. Additionally, most provinces are reluctant to extend assistance to families with working members. The employable-unemployable dichotomy is an entrenched feature of Canadian policy thinking: to be employable is to be ineligible for assistance, whatever the determination of the needs-test. With respect to the working poor, in short, the categorical approach persists. On the other hand, the 'need or likelihood of need' provision of the CAP legislation has itself proved an obstacle to the extension of assistance to the working poor, since it disallows cost-sharing for provincial programs that would provide assistance on the basis of, say, income rather than tested need. For all these reasons, and in spite of federal programs and such provincial measures as minimum wage laws and income supplementation plans, significant numbers of working Canadians remain in poverty, and their condition may grow worse in the future.

The federal government also sought to use CAP to improve social services in Canada, committing itself through the Plan to pay one-half of any increase in provincial expenditures on welfare services. The list of services eligible for cost-sharing is quite extensive; it includes rehabilitation services, casework, counselling, adoption services, day care, and homemaker services, as well as community development. Given the wide variety of services covered, it is not surprising that no discernible consensus has emerged regarding the role of social services in public policy. Should social services simply 'rehabilitate' the poor? Or should they be available on a universal basis? Should user charges be imposed? What is the effect of social services on poverty in Canada?

Access to services cost-shared under CAP is limited to the 'poor' population. Under CAP, social services were originally viewed as part of Canada's anti-poverty program – that is, as an effective instrument for improving the skills of disadvantaged individuals, thereby eliminating and preventing poverty. More recently, many observers have argued that some services ought to be universally available, since in many instances the income status of the individual using a given service is an irrelevant consideration. Furthermore, some services should be viewed not as private goods for consumption by the poor alone, but as public goods on the order of a collectively consumed item such as a public park, whose enjoyment by one individual does not detract from someone else's enjoyment. The related issue of user charges for social services is both topical and important (see Krashinsky 1981), but until there is some reliable way to separate private and public benefits there will be no easy rule to tell us if user charges should be levied and, if so, on which services and on what schedule. Yet any review of the CAP legislation must recognize these issues and attempt to deal with them.

CAP's failure to promote some semblance of national standards for provincial income assistance programs raises a major question of policy. Should there be national standards for provincial assistance programs? If standards are desirable, how can they be most effectively achieved in a federal state? CAP's failure to assist the working poor also raises some significant issues. Should income assistance be delivered on a categorical basis? More specifically, should the working poor constitute a separate group for income assistance, with separate eligibility regulations, delivery mechanisms, etc.? Or should we consider a different approach? Instead of a series of fragmented and complicated provincial assistance programs based on needs-testing, might we not consider an income maintenance system designed along the lines of a negative income tax or guaranteed annual income? This would involve a significant movement away from the current CAP emphasis on needs-testing towards income-tested programs. But here too there are a number of important policy issues – for example, which level of government would be better equipped to finance and administer such a program?

The Canada Assistance Plan is now under pressure on two fronts. Increasingly viewed as an inadequate basis for a comprehensive, integrated, and uniform assistance program, CAP is criticized by those interested in seeing an efficient and equitable social security system; and as a 'major' item in the federal budget it is seen as a possible candidate for any budget-slashing exercise. Adding to the general dissatisfaction is the federal government's perception that its present contributions to provincial assistance programs through CAP go largely unrecognized.

SCOPE AND APPROACH OF STUDY

This study is concerned with the Canada Assistance Plan and poverty. However, because it attempts to define the appropriate roles of the federal and the provincial governments in combating poverty, the study necessarily concerns itself as well with federal-provincial financial arrangements and social policies. Indeed, major cost-sharing arrangements such as the Canada Assistance Plan cannot be viewed apart from an intergovernmental perspective. The recognized starting point is the division of responsibilities between the federal and the provincial governments and their divergent tax powers; the general economic objective is to achieve a better match of responsibilities and tax capacities.

Federalism is essentially a political concept. The late Sir Kenneth Wheare defined the 'federal principle' as 'the method of dividing powers so that the general and regional governments are each, within a sphere, coordinate and independent' (Wheare 1963, 10).[2] Although many have offered other definitions, the common theme that emerges is that total domination of one government level by the other is incompatible with federalism. Consequently, it is impossible to understand what distinguishes federalism from other political structures without reference to the notion of divided or shared powers.

The task of economic analyses of federalism is to suggest which level of government can more appropriately conduct various economic functions. In Musgrave's now-famous distinction (Musgrave 1959, ch. 1), the central question is: should the central or the regional governments be given responsibility for the Allocation Branch of government? the Distribution Branch?[3] Economic analyses of federalism usually adopt either the common market approach or the fiscal federalism approach, both of which largely ignore the issue of distribution.

The common market view of federalism is almost exclusively concerned with allocative efficiency. The division of powers between levels of government is of concern only to the extent that some assignments may distort market patterns, inhibit mobility, and impede the flow of commodities more than others (Safarian 1974, 1980). Insofar as distributional considerations are taken into account, the emphasis is on regional disparities rather than individual incomes.

Fiscal federalism is also concerned principally with allocative efficiency, although in this case the focus is on public rather than private goods. The division of powers is seen in terms of ensuring that each level of government is charged with the functional responsibility for those public goods appropriate to its jurisdiction; that tax powers are adequate to finance the level of public goods demanded; and that the cost of public goods is borne as much as possible by those who benefit from them (Breton 1965, 1966; Weldon 1966; Oates 1972). Again the distributional issue is peripheral, and again the emphasis is on regional disparities.

In this study, however, federalism will be examined in terms of distribution, and the emphasis will be on the distribution of well-being among individuals, rather than among provinces or regions. We shall call this the social welfare

2 K.C. Wheare (1963, 17–20) regards the Canadian constitution as 'quasi-federal' because of the federal power of disallowance. In his view, this negates the 'classical federalism' principle of equal and autonomous status for both levels of government. J.R. Mallory (1965) describes various forms of Canadian federalism during the last century; in addition to 'quasi-federalism' and 'classical federalism', it is possible to discern 'emergency federalism', 'co-operative federalism', and 'double-image federalism'.

3 Musgrave identified three branches: Allocation, Distribution, and Stabilization. We ignore stabilization objectives except to note that it is conventionally assumed that stabilization activities are most appropriately carried out by the central authorities.

perspective.[4] In an economy with only private goods, income alone is a measure of an individual's access to resources. Hence, the level and distribution of income among individuals is a good indication of overall social welfare. Where public as well as private goods exist, the level of social welfare will also depend upon the supply and distribution of local and national public goods, mixed social goods, and merit goods.[5] But whatever the mix of goods, the problem of achieving a satisfactory level of social welfare is complicated in a federal state by the question of jurisdiction: should the power of redistribution be assigned to the central or the regional governments (Musgrave 1959; Oates 1968; Breton and Scott 1978; Usher 1978, 1980a,b; West and Winer 1980 a,b)? Consequently, distributional considerations should not be neglected in discussions of federalism.

The well-being of individuals is defined as the measure of their access to both income and available services. A social welfare perspective entails nothing more than an attempt to rank alternative distributions of well-being by some social evaluation function embodying ethical premises.[6] Although this study cannot propose a set of ethical premises necessary and sufficient to define the Canadian Just Society, it does focus on the distribution of well-being among individual Canadians and attempt to demonstrate how poverty and inequality may be reduced. It is our contention that CAP comprises programs whose redistributive function should be explicitly recognized. Indeed, redistribution is CAP's paramount concern, and so it is on the basis of redistribution that CAP should be assessed. Furthermore, income redistribution should be considered a national objective and federal-provincial relations should be patterned so as to facilitate

---

4 Nothing is gained by an elaborate definition of social welfare at this point, since our eventual concern will be with specific Canadian legislation and programs. A general definition of social welfare (policy) that approximates the concerns of this study is 'the policy of governments with regard to action having a direct impact on the welfare of citizens by providing them with services or income' (Marshall 1955, 7).

5 For a discussion of merit goods, see Musgrave (1959; 14). Head (1966, 1969), and McLure (1968). For a discussion of social goods and federalism, see Musgrave (1959; 179–83) and Scott (1964). For a discussion of mixed goods, see Weisbrod (1964). If the distribution of income is treated as a public good, then redistribution 'can be viewed as a social want, the satisfaction of which is generated in a manner similar to the satisfaction of other social wants' (Gillespie 1980, 177). Treating the distribution of income as a pure public good is an interesting metaphor; my approach here is to consider redistribution as a separate government function. See Thurow (1971) and Orr (1976) for a discussion of the income distribution as a pure public good.

6 Social evaluation functions represent ethical orderings of alternative income distributions. We use the term social welfare function to connote the more general concern with inequality. See Donaldson and Weymark (1980b).

the accomplishment of this end. From a social welfare perspective, federal-provincial divergences in tax powers and spending responsibilities must be viewed as institutional hurdles peculiar to federalism, to be somehow overcome in the orderly pursuit of national social welfare and income redistribution policies. This is not to say that provincial rights and the Constitution are mere inconveniences; the point is rather that one must look beyond federal-provincial arrangements and consider the common social welfare aims. In short, this study will review CAP from the perspective of the distribution of well-being among Canadians, who, under federalism, happen to live in various provinces.

The study is organized as follows. The following chapter provides a sketch of the division of federal and provincial powers with respect to social policy and discusses the historical background of the Canada Assistance Plan, its predecessor programs, and the negotiations leading up to the CAP legislation. The chapter also discusses reform attempts in the 1970s, particularly those initiatives associated with the Social Security Review which have affected programs cost-shared under CAP. Chapter 3 describes the Canada Assistance Plan legislation and its implementation and operation. Chapter 4 outlines a framework for the analysis of social welfare and redistributive policy issues within the context of federal structures. Its concerns are principally methodological; consequently, discussions of a more technical nature are confined to appendices. The issue of the working poor and the Canada Assistance Plan is considered in Chapter 5; this is followed, in Chapter 6, by a discussion of social services and CAP. The final chapter proposes a new financial arrangement to replace the present Canada Assistance Plan.

Our reform proposal attempts to address a number of important issues. These include: the lack of national standards for social assistance, the exclusion of the working poor from participation in assistance programs, and the failure to recognize the difference between the roles of assistance payments and social services. But there is a more fundamental flaw in the current cost-sharing arrangements. We believe that CAP is relatively disadvantageous to the poorer provinces and find it remarkable that there is no element of 'equalization' in the present formula. If the provinces and Canada are to cooperate in fighting poverty, some way of recognizing the relatively greater burden of the poorer provinces is essential.

Our proposals for revising CAP include: separate treatment of income assistance and social services, elimination of the needs-test in favour of income-testing, and the establishment of a new cost-sharing formula. This new formula would establish a standardized basic allowance for assistance programs, provide for a higher rate of federal contribution for poorer provinces up to some national minimum standard, and grant additional cost-sharing at some uniform rate thereafter. Our proposal is therefore firmly in the conditional cost-sharing tradition.

Obviously, proposals for reform do not arise in a political or economic vacuum. Proposals that imply an expansion of social programs and additional government expenditure are rarely popular, and never less so than during times of restraint. But the relevant considerations must surely be the large number of Canadians who are in poverty and the inadequacy of the benefit levels in provincial assistance programs. Furthermore, federal expenditures through CAP are relatively insignificant – less than 1 per cent of GNE and less than 4 per cent of total federal outlays. For what was heralded as a 'landmark' development in Canada's social security system this is surely not much.

It is appropriate at this point to add a few words about the limits of the present study. Part II of the Canada Assistance Plan contains arrangements concerning Indian welfare; because no agreements between Canada and the provinces have ever been signed under this portion of the legislation, the chapters to follow do not consider the problems of Indian welfare – not because these problems are unimportant, but rather because CAP has had no effect in this area and solutions must be sought elsewhere than by amending this portion of the act. Part III of CAP deals with special work activity projects; since each work activity project approved is a special case, the present study does not examine this aspect of the CAP legislation either. Finally, the study does not deal with provincial-municipal financial arrangements in the area of social assistance and social services.

2
Federal-provincial relations and the Canada Assistance Plan: a brief history

This chapter describes the distribution between the federal and provincial governments of powers and responsibilities relevant to social policy. It also reviews federal welfare programs previous to the Canada Assistance Plan, provides a brief account of the negotiations leading up to the Plan, and discusses the subsequent efforts to replace the plan with an even more comprehensive formula for social assistance – efforts that culminated in the Social Security Review of the mid-1970s.

DIVISION OF POWERS AND EARLY SOCIAL WELFARE RESPONSIBILITIES

The division of powers between the federal government and the provinces was originally defined in the British North America Act. Section 91 of the BNA Act detailed specific federal powers and also gave parliament authority to make laws for '... the Peace, Order and Good Government of Canada in relation to all Matters not coming within the Classes of Subjects ... assigned exclusively to ... the Provinces.' Moreover, the federal government received what were at the time the most significant sources of revenue (that is, customs and excise taxes[1]) as well as unlimited powers of taxation.[2] In short, the major functional responsibilities of government – and the financial resources to carry them out – were to reside with

1 The Maritime Provinces derived 80 per cent or more of their revenue in 1866 from customs and made virtually no attempt to levy excise taxes. The Province of Canada derived 66 per cent of its revenue from customs and 17 per cent from excise taxes. (Smiley/Rowell-Sirois Report 1963, 48–9.)
2 Section 91(3) of the BNA Act gives the parliament of Canada authority over 'the Raising of Money by any Mode or System of Taxation'. Provinces were limited by Section 92(2) to 'Direct taxation within the province in order to the raising of a revenue for provincial purposes'. The distinction between direct and indirect taxes was established in Bank of Toronto v. Lambe, 1887. See Russell (1965, 145–52).

the national government.

Section 92 of the BNA Act defined the areas in which the provinces were to have exclusive jurisdiction. Provincial responsibilities included what are now customarily referred to as the social policy functions, including education and health care.[3] At the time of Confederation, however, these functions were regarded as largely a municipal concern. Therefore provincial expenditures (and revenues) would not have to be very great; indeed, provincial burdens were actually expected to decline as municipal institutions expanded (Smiley/Rowell-Sirois Report 1963, 56–57; Moore, Perry, and Beach 1966).

This lack of commitment to social welfare by the higher levels of government derived from two sources: the social philosophy of the Confederation era and the legacy of the Elizabethan Poor Laws. The social welfare function of government was then regarded as a 'residual' one, meaning that charity was, in the first place, the responsibility of the family, the church, or private organizations. Only upon the failure of all other avenues of support would government intervene, and such aid was to be minimal and restricted solely to those truly in need as determined by the administration of a means or needs test.[4] The second important influence, the tradition of the Elizabethan Poor Laws, dictated that public welfare should be in the hands of the lowest level of government. Thus, while the provinces would have ultimate jurisdiction over social policy – to the extent that this was a function of government at all – practical responsibility for such policy would rest with local government.

This arrangement did not prove an enduring one. Changes in social philosophy and growing demand for public welfare services eventually magnified the importance of provincial responsibility for social welfare far beyond the expectations of the designers of Confederation. On the other hand, the constitutional

---

3 The sections of the BNA Act giving responsibility for social policy (other than education) to the provinces are 92(7), (8), (13) and (16):
   (7)   The Establishment, Maintenance and Management of Hospitals, Asylums, Charities, and Eleemosynary Institutions in and for the Province ...
   (8)   Municipal Institutions in the Province.
   (13) Property and Civil Rights in the Province.
   (16) Generally all Matters of a merely local or private nature.
4 In social programs, receipt of benefits may be subject to a means, income, or needs test. With means-testing, eligibility to receive benefits is determined by the income and assets available to the individual. Income-testing is similar to means-testing but applies to income only. Needs-testing takes into account not only the resources available to the individual or family, but an assessment of need as well. Universal programs do not require a means, income, or needs test.

denial to the provinces of significant revenues and powers of taxation made it difficult for them to adequately carry out an enlarged welfare function. This misalignment of resources and responsibilities between the federal and provincial governments was the inevitable result of federalism in a context of economic and social change. May (1969, 55) writes:

If all functions – expenditure-incurring and revenue-raising – are allocated between the two levels of governments according to which level can carry them out most efficiently, or simply on the basis of which functions one level is prepared to give up, there is no reason at all why expenditure obligations and revenue sources should balance at either level. Even if there was an initial balance, changes in economic conditions and new demands for public services would be bound to upset the balance.

In order to deal with this imbalance, the provinces and the federal government entered into a variety of cost-sharing arrangements. However, in the absence of a well-defined framework for accommodation between the two levels of government, progress in the creation of national social policy was tentative and slow. For example, although the first significant shared-cost program, the Old Age Pension, was introduced in 1927,[5] it was not until 1936 that all the provinces and territories were participants, and not until 1948 that revisions were made to ensure some measure of uniformity (Guest 1980, 76–78). In fact, at the end of the Second World War, only two social welfare programs were provided on a national and uniform basis – Unemployment Insurance and Family Allowances. Other social programs were left to provincial governments and consequently varied widely across the country. Moreover, provincial programs developed prior to the Second World War were usually *ad hoc* responses to emergency situations: in general, provincial governments lacked both the will and the resources to establish coherent social policies on a permanent basis.

During the post-war period, demand for social programs grew at an unprecedented rate, yet the dilemma posed by the initial allocation of revenues and responsibilities persisted: the provinces lacked the resources and the federal

5 Earlier cost-sharing programs were limited in duration or involved minor amounts. Conditional grants were first used in 1914 under the Agricultural Instruction Act to provide federal assistance for agricultural education over a ten-year period. The first grant on a continuing basis was in 1918 and related to the financing of provincial employment offices. The federal government began demanding certain minimal standards of performance with the Canada Highways Act (1919) and the Technical Education Act (1919). The indispensible reference for old age pensions in Canada is Bryden (1974).

government lacked the constitutional authority to meet this demand. The only solution, short of amending the constitution, was an increase in transfers of revenue to the provinces. The result was federal collaboration with the provinces in a wide variety of welfare programs, with many gaps and inconsistencies in coverage. Nevertheless, the federal government sought with some success to use its command of resources to create a uniform national social welfare policy – an effort that culminated in its introduction of the Canada Assistance Plan.

ASSISTANCE PROGRAMS PRIOR TO CAP

The Canada Assistance Plan was first mentioned in the 1965 Speech from the Throne as one element of an ambitious five-part program to eliminate poverty in Canada.[6] The Plan was a major addition to the arsenal of cost-shared programs used by the federal government to influence policy in areas of provincial jurisdiction. Its focus was on social assistance – the most basic of anti-poverty programs. The Plan encouraged the provinces to integrate diverse assistance measures into single comprehensive programs. It offered increased federal support for program expansion and provided significant incentives for the improvement of welfare services. The federal government believed that CAP would introduce order and consistency to the cluttered, and often disjointed, provincial public assistance systems.

The Canada Assistance Plan directly affected several cost-shared assistance programs already in place. These programs were embodied in four pieces of federal legislation: the Old Age Assistance Act, the Blind Persons Act, the Disabled Persons Act, and the Unemployment Assistance Act. Their common objective was income support for those least able to provide for themselves. The federal government shared the costs of the programs; the provinces administered them and made payments on a means- or needs-tested basis. The programs were categorical and directed principally to individuals not in the labour force. It was implicitly assumed that employment policies, unemployment insurance, and old age security programs would cover the needs of the remaining population. Consequently, the programs did not provide benefits for individuals either chronically unemployed or employed but earning low incomes – sometimes referred to as the working poor.

The Old Age Assistance Act came into effect with the 1952 federal revisions to its 1927 Old Age Pensions Act. Two complementary pieces of legislation – the

6 The other parts of the program were concerned with regional and rural development, manpower policy, urban renewal, and the Company of Young Canadians.

Old Age Security Act and the Old Age Assistance Act – were introduced. The Old Age Security Act established, for the first time, a universal pension plan in Canada. The program was federally administered (due to Section 94 A of the BNA Act) and provided a flat rate pension to all persons 70 years of age or over, subject to a residency requirement of 20 years immediately preceding commencement of benefits. The Old Age Assistance Act introduced a cost-shared program of the 'traditional' type. The federal government paid half the costs incurred by provincial programs for financial assistance to persons between 65 and 70 years of age provided that such assistance was granted subject to a means test and a residency requirement.

In 1965, it was decided to lower the eligibility age for Old Age Security to 65, not immediately, but gradually over a five-year period. The Old Age Assistance Program became unnecessary at the end of 1969, when all those qualifying for Old Age Assistance benefits could now receive the universal Old Age Security. During 1965–69, when Old Age Assistance payments were being phased out, the Canada Assistance Plan came into effect. Consequently, the Old Age Assistance Program was included among those programs which could be incorporated into CAP by the provinces.

The second piece of legislation affected by CAP was the Blind Persons Act. When first introduced, in 1937, pensions for the blind were incorporated in the Old Age Pensions Act. Eligibility was restricted to those 40 years of age or older (reduced in 1947 to 21), and, as with Old Age Assistance, there was a 20-year residency requirement. With the passage of the Blind Persons Act of 1951, the federal government assumed 75 per cent of the cost of provincial allowances paid to blind persons on a means-tested basis. Assistance under the Blind Persons Act ended when the recipient became eligible for Old Age Security. The residency requirement of the act was subsequently reduced to 10 years, and in 1955 the eligible age was lowered to 18.

Social assistance to the disabled was also provided through federal-provincial cost-sharing arrangements prior to CAP. The Allowances for Disabled Persons Act (1954) provided a means-tested, income-security program for the 'totally and permanently disabled' over 18 and resident in Canada for 10 years prior to receiving benefits (Statistics Canada 1978, 290–92). The Vocational Rehabilitation of Disabled Persons Act (1952), on the other hand, was a social service program emphasizing the vocational rehabilitation of physically and mentally disabled individuals. The program's aim was to facilitate the entry of disabled persons into the work force, and to that end it provided medical, social, and vocational assessment, counselling, training, maintenance allowances, prostheses, tools, books, and equipment. Accordingly, the rehabilitation program had neither a residency requirement nor a means-test and covered all individuals over the provincially determined school-leaving age. In 1961, the two programs were consolidated under the Vocational Rehabilitation of Disabled Persons Act.

Unemployment assistance was initially proposed in 1945 as part of the federal government's post-war reconstruction plans and was to be financed and administered in conjunction with the Unemployment Insurance Program. However, the federal and provincial governments failed to agree on a formula for collaboration until 1956, when Parliament passed the Unemployment Assistance Act. The act provided for federal cost-sharing of provincially and municipally administered unemployment assistance programs. However, federal contributions came into effect only when the number of persons assisted exceeded .45 per cent of the provincial population. Intended to ensure that federal funds were used only to assist the employable unemployed, this provision was removed in 1957 (CAP Annual Report 1968–69, 6), which meant the federal government was now cost-sharing assistance to employables and unemployables alike. Unlike previous assistance programs, Unemployment Assistance did not impose a ceiling on the amount of assistance or the allowable income of a recipient. Neither was there an age or residency requirement. Cost-sharing was on a 50-50 basis and excluded administrative costs.

The Unemployment Assistance Act of 1956 was, in retrospect, clearly a bridge between the Canada Assistance Plan and its predecessor assistance programs. Up until then, the federal and provincial governments had established programs which highlighted certain readily identifiable characteristics of potential recipients. It was not enough to be poor and in need; one also had to belong to a special category or 'deserving group' such as the elderly, the blind, or the totally and permanently disabled. These categorical programs were also restrictive in that low ceilings were placed on benefit levels and the means-test was applied in a strict manner.[7]

In contrast, assistance under the Unemployment Assistance Act was not tied to individual characteristics, and a needs-test rather than a means-test was the basis for establishing assistance levels. Although the program did remain in the categorical tradition, since it confined eligibility to the unemployed, its extension of assistance to unemployed employables laid the groundwork for the adoption of a single assistance measure. In addition, the use of a needs-test and the choice of the family rather than the individual as the basic unit for determining the amount of assistance marked a growing recognition of the importance of need as a basis for social assistance. Although far from comprehensive, the

7 For example, of approximately 100,000 people between the ages of 18 and 64 classified as either severely or totally disabled and having no or little income of their own, only 31,825 received allowances under the Disabled Persons Act (Guest 1980, 146).

Unemployment Assistance Program nevertheless foreshadowed the Canada Assistance Plan.

NEGOTIATION AND FORMULATION OF CAP

The early 1960s brought growing dissatisfaction with the cost-shared categorical social assistance programs. Criticism centred on the narrow nature of the definitions in the various acts, on the income ceilings and the constraints on allowable income, and particularly on the eligibility restrictions. An individual had to be 'totally and permanently disabled', or blind, or elderly, to receive benefits under the Disabled Persons Act, the Blind Persons Act, or the Old Age Assistance Act. Although Unemployment Assistance was not quite as restrictive, recipients still had to be unemployed. Another major criticism concerned the inflexibility of the programs in regard to the different needs of recipients. Inflexibility was also apparent in the tendency to concentrate on assistance to individuals rather than to families in need. It was generally felt that the categorical nature of the programs focused on the 'cause, rather than the fact, of need' (Guest 1980, 156). Further, the separation of assistance on a categorical basis led to unwieldy administration and uncoordinated programs. Adding to the discontent over the inadequacies of the existing programs was a rising public concern over poverty and inequality of opportunity in Canada. The provinces were united in demanding greater financial assistance from the federal government.

The need to consolidate public assistance programs was mentioned during the federal-provincial first ministers conference held in September 1963 to discuss the Canada Pension Plan. Following a second conference in November 1963, a federal-provincial working group of deputy ministers was established to review existing cost-shared welfare programs. The principal recommendation of the working group, made public in 1964, was that the federal and provincial governments 'work towards an integrated, comprehensive general assistance program based on meeting need' (cited in CAP Annual Report 1970–71, 5). A further recommendation came from the provincial ministers of welfare 'that the federal government share fully in the costs of mothers' allowances, health services and administration' (*Ibid.*). A second meeting of welfare ministers in 1964 approved the basic features of a new, integrated joint welfare program. In early 1966, the provincial welfare ministers recommended that benefits be extended to children and youths in the care of welfare authorities. After intensive but harmonious federal-provincial consultation, the Canada Assistance Plan Act was introduced in the House of Commons as Bill C-1 on April 4, 1966, approved by the Senate on July 12, and given Royal Assent on July 23, 1966. The act was made retroactive to April 1 of the same year. The Canada Assistance Plan was hailed by many as a landmark development in the history of Canada's social security system.

The formulation of CAP has generally been viewed as a highly successful instance of federal-provincial negotiation. Previous negotiations, such as those over the Canada Pension Plan, had been marked by conflict and disagreement, but in the case of CAP there was substantial consultation and collaboration between the provinces and the federal government from the start.[8] The federal response to provincial demands for more cost-sharing and greater flexibility was 'prompt and generous'. Thus it was swiftly agreed, for example, that the federal government should participate in mothers' allowances. This readiness to oblige had both a bureaucratic and a political aspect. Federal officials accepted that larger federal contributions would be required for a more effective, comprehensive, and consolidated welfare system, and they were anxious to try innovative programs. As well, officials in Indian Affairs wanted a better welfare program for the country's native population. The congenial atmosphere was also partly due to the 'old social work school ties' of many officials (Dyck 1976; Splane 1977; Bella 1977, 1979). Finally, federal officials seemed to realize that their provincial counterparts were generally more experienced in welfare administration. At the political level, the Pearson government, then in its early years, was reluctant to create friction by rejecting provincial proposals for increased assistance for welfare programs. Moreover, as negotiations progressed, the federal cabinet's interest in CAP increased. Cooperation between the two levels of government ranged from the simple exchange of information to federal expansion of the Plan to accommodate provincial programs not covered by the original proposals.

The one major objection to CAP came from Quebec, which opted out; however, Quebec eventually signed a financing agreement under which it received funds from Ottawa for programs normally covered under CAP. The other provinces lobbied for more flexibility than the existing four cost-shared programs allowed. The federal government agreed to greater provincial flexibility but retained its belief that strong federal control was necessary for an effective national welfare program. In this instance the participants struck their traditional postures with respect to federal-provincial relations and social policy, but even so the issue was amiably resolved.

---

8 The rest of this section is drawn mainly from Dyck (1976). Bella (1979) also characterizes the negotiations as cordial but attributes this to federal concessions to provincial initiatives.

Two additional opportunities for falling-out arose prior to the implementation of CAP. First, the provinces demanded greater federal funding for child welfare, and after some pressure the federal government agreed. Second, the Atlantic Provinces demanded a differential cost-sharing formula based on provincial need. The richer provinces objected, and the federal government held fast to the original 50–50 cost-sharing formula, feeling that regional differences could be accommodated by equalization payments.

PRELUDE TO THE SOCIAL SECURITY REVIEW

The negotiations that produced the Canada Assistance Plan may have been a model of federal-provincial harmony, yet within two years the Plan itself came under attack as an inadequate response to the problem of poverty in Canada. In 1968, the Senate Committee on Poverty (the Croll Committee) was given a mandate to investigate all aspects of poverty and to recommend effective policy measures. The committee's report was uncompromisingly critical of CAP and the public assistance systems consolidated under it. The committee recommended that they be scrapped and replaced by a guaranteed annual income scheme (Canada 1971, Section Two).

This recommendation met with considerable resistance. The federal government, in the middle of discussions involving constitutional reform, had already declared its position in a widely publicized working paper, *Income Security and Social Services* (Canada 1969), and it was reluctant to introduce another contentious issue to the bargaining table. Also, the minister of National Health and Welfare had only recently completed an internal review of the social security system. Significantly, the product of that review, the White Paper on *Income Security for Canadians* (Canada 1970), had come out in favour of a more selective approach than that proposed by the Senate Committee. Consequently, the Senate Committee's recommendation was never taken seriously.

Between 1968 and 1971, federal and provincial leaders met several times to discuss constitutional reform. Social security issues emerged as a major point of contention. The federal position was clear – a strong federal presence in the social security field was both necessary and desirable (Canada 1969). Quebec, on the other hand, pushed for greater provincial control over social policy, arguing that the federal government was the main obstacle to the implementation of a comprehensive social security system. Discussion reached an impasse, and neither the federal nor the provincial governments emerged from the Victoria Conference in 1971 in a position to implement a truly comprehensive, integrated social security system.

Yet the conviction persisted at both levels of government that such a system was necessary, and that CAP would have to be amended or replaced. The search for an appropriate formula was renewed in the Federal-Provincial Review of Social Security, initiated in 1973. The Review failed in the sense that it did not lead to any changes in CAP; indeed, the original legislation is still in force today. Nonetheless, the Review did yield important results, especially in the areas of income maintenance policy and social services strategy.[9]

THE INCOME MAINTENANCE COMPONENT

The Social Security Review established working parties of technical advisers. The terms of reference for one such group, the Working Party on Income Maintenance (WPIM), included policy and design issues related to the establishment of a comprehensive and coordinated income maintenance system. WPIM's initial meeting, held in July 1973, gave priority to Family Allowances and the Canada Pension Plan.

WPIM's role was not to initiate policy but to assess the technical feasibility of policies agreed upon by the federal and provincial welfare ministers. In September 1973, the Conference of Welfare Ministers announced certain changes to the Canada/Quebec Pension Plans and the Family Allowances Program. It had been agreed to increase CPP/QPP benefits and to index payments. Family Allowances were nearly tripled, indexed, and made subject to taxation. Provinces were permitted to vary the level of payments on the basis of age of child or family size so long as the average payment per child was $20 and the minimum payment $12. This was a radical innovation, viewed at the time as a concession to gain Quebec's support for the Review (Van Loon 1979, 486). Subsequently, almost every province developed (or at least announced an intention to develop) unilateral changes in its social assistance programs. Some provinces also proceeded with totally new income supplementation programs.

---

9 The significance of the Social Security Review warrants much broader treatment than can be given here. Former Deputy Minister of National Welfare A.W. Johnson (1975) gives an account of events up to 1975; Splane (1977) and Doyle (1978) describe the review up to the time of Bill C-57; Guest (1980, ch. 12) provides a more complete historical treatment; Hum (1980a) comments on unanswered technical questions raised by the review and its relation to the experimental NIT project; Ryant (1980) examines the review as a case study of federal-provincial consultation; and Van Loon (1979) provides an analysis of the political process. My understanding of events is also taken from the technical background papers, the official communiqués of ministers, and conversations with certain individuals involved with the review.

The ministers now instructed WPIM to concentrate on the development of an integrated income support and supplementation program. Of six alternative approaches developed by WPIM, three were income-tested plans (Options 1, 2, 3), and three were child-related programs (Options 4, 5, 6). All the options were to be coordinated with social insurance programs and integrated with the tax system. The ministers rejected the child-related options and requested WPIM to study the design characteristics and cost implications of the income-tested options. The first option was a single guaranteed income system with eligibility based solely on income. The second and third options proposed a two-tier, but integrated system; eligibility for the higher level of support would be restricted by an employment availability test. The difference between the second and third options concerned the method of delivery: support would be provided through either transfer payments or refundable tax credits. Meeting in November 1974, the welfare ministers agreed that levels of support could vary across the country, that any work-eligibility test should, if possible, be 'objective', that 'Ministers of Finance would have to play a major role within their respective governments', and 'that a modified Canada Assistance Plan could be employed as a vehicle for achieving the reforms Ministers favoured (in particular Options 1 and 2), or entirely new legislation could be introduced' (Communiqué, November 19, 20, 1974, 13).

From this point onward, the Review lost momentum. A federal cabinet committee favoured a two-tier system,[10] while the NDP governments of British Columbia, Manitoba, and Saskatchewan – and, initially, the government of Quebec – favoured a single-tier program. Eventually, in April 1975, the welfare ministers agreed on the basic outline of a new guaranteed income scheme. The program would have two components: income support for those 'unable to work or for whom employment cannot be found' and income supplementation with 'built-in work incentives' for those 'who are working but whose incomes are inadequate'. Support levels would be set by the provinces, and the federal government was 'prepared to increase substantially its financial contribution, over the 50 per cent which now applies to provincial assistance programs, by paying two-thirds of the supplementation component of the guaranteed income system'. The 'detailed operational design' of this new guaranteed income system would still have to be negotiated and it was understood by all that 'guidelines relating to the federal sharing of provincial assistance programs under the Canada Assistance Plan [will have to] apply for [this] interim period while the operational design for the income support and supplementation system is being developed'

10 My account of what went on in cabinet is drawn entirely from Van Loon (1979, 493–98).

(Communiqué, April 30, May 1, 1975, 4–5). The Canada Assistance Plan was on its way to being phased out.

However, although the income support and supplementation proposal had been approved by cabinet committee, the full cabinet merely agreed with the 'concept' and stated that the program would have to be 'delayed', meaning that it was all but dead. In the following year, the cabinet approved a pared-down version of the program, with eligibility restricted to families with children and to those aged 55 to 65, and costing $240 million instead of $2 billion. This proposal, presented to the provinces in February 1976, received general (if tepid) support but was rejected by Ontario and consequently abandoned.

The Social Security Review was an attempt to direct the welfare system away from the 'assistance plans' typified by the Canada Assistance Plan and towards 'income and employment' plans (Communiqué, November 19, 20, 1974, 1). The Review did encourage new provincial legislation in the area of income and employment, and it also brought about an expansion of existing federal income schemes. Yet it must be remembered that the expected result of the review process was new federal legislation – indeed, many of the new provincial programs had been introduced in anticipation of such legislation (Ryant 1980, 9). By this criterion the Review failed, since no new delivery systems were introduced; nor was the legislative basis for cost-sharing under the Canada Assistance Plan changed.

THE SOCIAL SERVICES COMPONENT

The Working Party on Social Services (WPSS) was largely made up of social workers and social service administrators. The prevailing assumption at the beginning of the Review was that social services were to be treated as ancillary to employment and income maintenance programs; this was the role traditionally assigned to social services by economists, political scientists, and public finance experts, who dominated the Review. But it was social services, and not the income support and supplementation proposals, that emerged as the central agenda item towards the end of the review process.

The task of the Working Party on Social Services was to prepare an inventory of social and employment services, evaluate existing levels of services, and identify methods to improve delivery, coordination, and extension.[11] WPSS's

---

11 Kelly (1977) writes that from the outset this working party took as its mandate an examination of all public social services irrespective of their relatedness to employment functions; it wanted to rethink the broad objectives of the social services. However, the 'descent from ideals to practical realities tended to be difficult for this working party'.

analysis was 'largely descriptive' and 'loosely formulated', and it evoked little interest when the group presented its first and last report in 1975 (Ryant 1980, 12).

WPSS's original mandate confined it to the study of current cost-sharing arrangements (Doyle 1978, 31). The working party was asked to 'develop alternative legislative frameworks for the delivery and financing of social services' and 'to examine specifically the question of cost-sharing arrangements for specific kinds of service programs, and to review current problems in the interpretation of the Canada Assistance Plan Act and regulations' (Communiqué, November 19, 20, 1974, 5).[12] However, persistent objections to the financing provisions of the Canada Assistance Plan, particularly the limiting of services to those 'in need or likely to become in need', led the federal government to announce 'a sweeping change in the approach to the financing and development of social services in Canada' (Communiqué, April 30, 1975, 1). The CAP arrangements for cost-sharing on the basis of 'need or likely need' would be replaced; new legislation would be introduced dividing services into (five) categories according to target groups; sharing would be on a straight 50 per cent basis; extending rehabilitation and support services for the aged and the handicapped would become a priority; and graduated user charges would be introduced (*Ibid.*, 2–4). The new social services legislation was to be in place by early 1976.

Both the timing and substance of this initiative deserve to be noted. In 1975, the income maintenance strategy was beginning to lose momentum and a new focus was required to salvage the Review. Therefore, 'early in 1975, the federal deputy minister and his senior advisor on Social Service programs sat down virtually alone and very rapidly drafted a proposed outline for a new cost sharing arrangement [for social services]' (Van Loon 1979, 488). The previously ignored report of the Working Party on Social Services had recommended that social services be made available to all, but on a free, subsidized, or full-cost basis according to income. The report addressed the narrow issues of service categories and graduated user charges, but not federal-provincial cost-sharing or administrative arrangements (Ryant 1980, 14). Consequently, the report was of 'extremely limited utility' for designing a new cost-sharing arrangement and

12 A separate report dealing with possible changes to the federal-provincial agreements on the Vocational Rehabilitation of Disabled Persons was also considered at this meeting. The federal government announced that it would extend the existing VRDP agreements for another year, at which time it was hoped that 'the federal-provincial social security review would have reached agreement on the longer run approach to the social service system, including rehabilitation services' (Communiqué, November 19, 20, 1974, 5).

led to a 'technically inept' and ill-received legislative draft (*Ibid.*, 15). What followed was a series of negotiations over nearly two years, nine legislative outlines, and fourteen federal drafts. A federal ultimatum to 'take it or leave it', accompanied by a threat to terminate CAP cost-sharing at the end of the legal notice period, eventually brought the provinces to accept the new proposal, which became Bill C-57 or the Social Services Act (Van Loon 1979, 489; Johnson 1975, 463; Ryant 1980, 12, 14–16).

Bill C-57 was to replace the social services portion of Part I of the Canada Assistance Plan Act, to repeal those sections of the act concerning Indian welfare (Part II), and to repeal completely the Vocational Rehabilitation of Disabled Persons Act. The bill received first reading on June 20, 1977 but was allowed to die on the parliamentary order paper. However, the policy direction of the intended legislation deserves mention.

Bill C-57 was designed to 'strengthen and consolidate the status of social services as a sector which is independent of public assistance and which has relevance in one way or another to practically all Canadians' (Canada. Department of National Health and Welfare, 1978, 2). Thus, unlike the Canada Assistance Plan, Bill C-57 recognized that social services were for not only the poor but potentially everyone. This is clear from the comprehensive definition of social services adopted in the act. Social services were defined as:

services having as their object: enabling persons to lead useful, satisfying and independent lives; preventing personal and social conditions that cause disadvantage or disability; raising individuals, families, and groups to a higher level of participation in social and economic life; protecting those whose personal or social well being is at risk; or developing individual, group and community capacity for growth, enrichment and social participation. (Canada, Social Services Act, 2)

The services to be financed under the act included crisis intervention services, information and referral services, meal services, employment related services, transportation services for the disabled, children's services, rehabilitation services, social integration services, day care services for children and adults, home support services, counselling services, and certain developmental and preventive services to communities. The legislation also attempted to achieve a balance between services to individuals (such as family counselling) and services to the general public – including those to be used at user option (such as information and referral services) and those open to users of defined status (such as transportation services for the disabled).

The act contained arrangements for 50–50 cost-sharing of eligible services. Significantly, the act treated provincial grants to voluntary agencies supplying eligible services and direct payments to individuals for the purchase of social services exactly the same as expenses incurred directly by the province.

The legislation also called for the introduction of user charges for certain types of services (day care for children and adults, home support services, meal services, counselling services, and employment services) and left open the option of introducing user charges for other services as well. The regulations of the proposed Social Services Act contained user charge guidelines based on income. The provinces were given the option to ignore or to modify this fee schedule, but federal contributions would be based on the expenditure a province would have incurred had the guidelines been followed. The provinces originally supported the Social Services Act as an advance over CAP (in that it allowed much greater flexibility in the design of programs) but raised a number of important administrative and jurisdictional issues during the summer following its introduction in the Commons.

In August 1977, the federal Minister of Health and Welfare announced that Bill C-57 would be replaced by Bill C-55 and unconditional block-funding. Each provincial government would be given a grant in lieu of cost-sharing for social services, with no provision that such funds need be spent for social service programs. The provinces had not been consulted about this proposal, and a number of provincial welfare ministers were displeased, but not surprised, by the announcement. Provincial governments had come to feel that cost-sharing distorted provincial priorities. Moreover, it was known that the federal government wanted greater cost control and more predictability in its expenditures. In any case, block-funding had already been applied to medical insurance;[13] it did not seem unusual to apply it now to social services.[14] Under Bill C-55, the federal government's contribution would be determined by a formula which took into account the amount of money the province received in 1977–78 for social services under the Canada Assistance Plan and the Vocational Rehabilitation of Disabled Persons Act (and, in some provinces, the Youth Offender Agreements). An additional $150 million was to be added to the block fund in 1979 and an escalator clause based on the growth in Gross National Product and in population was planned.

Critics of Bill C-55 argued that the social services, unlike the 'established' hospital and medical care programs, were immature and in the 'developmental' stage. They expressed a number of concerns, two of which are particularly important. First, it was claimed that block funding would take away one of the

13 See Van Loon (1978) for a discussion of the politics underlying this initiative.
14 For a sampling of reaction from the social work profession, see Kelly (1977), Riches (1977), and Norquay (1979).

key arguments traditionally used by community groups, social agencies, and welfare ministers to persuade provincial cabinets to increase social expenditures: namely, that under cost-sharing the federal government would pick up one-half the cost of any increase. Second, there was concern that the provinces might use the federal transfers in areas other than social services (e.g., public works), and that minimum national standards might be eroded.

Not all provinces supported the block funding offer, but eventually, under strong pressure from the federal government, a reluctant consensus was reached. It appeared in mid-1978 that Bill C-55, the Social Services Financing Act, would receive certain passage. However, in August the prime minister announced a series of restraint measures, including a reduction of projected federal expenditures. Proposed programs, as opposed to those protected by legislative guarantees, were especially vulnerable. Bill C-55 would have increased federal expenditures in its first year of operation by $61 million over the estimated $516 million cost of the CAP and VRDP programs. The federal contribution under Bill C-55 was projected to rise by an additional $221 million in the second year and to reach $1.9 billion in 1987 (Health and Welfare Canada, 1978). The federal welfare minister, Marc Lalonde, finally announced that Bill C-55 was dead; its death was due partly to reductions in federal expenditures dictated by events outside the review process (Van Loon 1979, 491) and partly to provincial objections and deteriorating federal-provincial relations (Ryant 1980, 17). Despite numerous negotiations, much compromise, and two bills, the social services provisions of the 1966 Canada Assistance Plan Act remain.

CONCLUSION

Although no dramatic developments in social security emerged during the 1970s, several incremental changes did occur. One such change affected the federal-provincial agreements covering supplementary nursing home care benefits signed with Ontario, Manitoba, and Alberta to compensate for revenues forgone when universal nursing home care benefits were introduced. These agreements were superceded by the new Federal-Provincial Fiscal Arrangements and Established Programs Financing Act of 1977, which authorized the federal government to make a per capita payment to provinces to cover costs of certain types of adult institutional care, home care services, and ambulatory health care services provided by the provinces. The extension of the FPFA-EPF Act to cover nursing home care and adult residential care services had a major impact on the 'homes for special care' provisions of the Canada Assistance Plan. Whereas CAP previously shared in the total cost of maintaining needy adults in such institutions, CAP-sharing is now limited to the current Old Age Security/Guaranteed Income Supplement maximum for a single individual. Another development in federal-provincial relations respecting social policy was the concluding of agreements with New Brunswick and Ontario to permit federal contributions toward the cost of services to young offenders. In other provinces, where young offenders are under the control of child welfare authorities rather than correctional authorities, these services are cost-shared under CAP.

Provincial governments also introduced new policy initiatives. In 1973, British Columbia introduced an income supplement program to bring the income of wage earners up to at least the level received under social assistance. Ontario embarked on a similar scheme in 1975. In 1974, Saskatchewan implemented its Family Income Plan (FIP), which provided monthly payments to families with dependent children under 18. FIP was a product of expectations raised by the Federal-Provincial Social Security Review; it was placed in jeopardy when the Review failed to produce new legislation to replace the Canada Assistance Plan. Today, about 75 per cent of FIP is eligible for cost-sharing under the assistance provisions of CAP.

Although the tangible accomplishments of the Social Security Review itself were few, some changes did result – for example, changes in Family Allowances and CPP/QPP. The Child Tax Credit might also be included in this list. Less tangibly, the Review brought improved federal-provincial communication, as well as increased understanding of income supplementation alternatives and tax credits. With respect to income maintenance, there was considerable movement away from the needs-testing orientation of the Canada Assistance Plan towards income-tested alternatives. The Review also stimulated a clear movement away from the view that social services should be reserved for those 'in need or likely to be in need', the current basis for cost-sharing under the Canada Assistance Plan. Because of the Review, the principles of universal availability and income-tested graduated user fees for social services were almost adopted. Rehabilitative services received more attention and, perhaps most significant of all, social services came to be viewed as 'essential' in their own right and divorced from income maintenance.[15]

15 The Working Party on Community Employment requires a brief mention. It was to catalogue programs aimed at assisting individuals who had been unemployed for an extended period, examine government direct job-creation programs, and prepare a set of policy proposals for an employment strategy. Ministers eventually agreed to examine proposals to assist those with particular and continuing difficulty in getting and keeping employment. This strategy threatened existing practices and programs, and fostered tension and conflict between the Department of Manpower and Immigration and the Department of National Health and Welfare. The working party merely submitted a 'framework for development'. Ministers agreed to initiate twenty experimental employment projects across Canada 'to gain broader experience' (Communiqué, November 19, 20, 1974, 4). The federal cabinet approved an expenditure of $50 million over 1974–77 for this purpose, but few projects got beyond the planning stage. Funding disappeared with the 1978 budget cuts and with it all traces of the Community Employment strategy.

3
The Canada Assistance Plan: description and operation

The Canada Assistance Plan dramatically expanded the scope of federal involvement in social policy. In addition to encouraging an integration of assistance programs, CAP extended cost-sharing to a wide variety of social services and to most costs of administration incurred by provincial welfare agencies. This chapter describes the structure of the CAP legislation and outlines how CAP has operated since its inception.

STRUCTURE OF THE CANADA ASSISTANCE PLAN ACT

The Canada Assistance Plan is divided into three main parts. The first part concerns general assistance and social services, the second part deals with Indian welfare, and the third part covers work-activity projects. Separate federal-provincial agreements are permitted for each part, allowing the provinces considerable flexibility in the choice and the timing of programs.

Part I of the CAP legislation sought to replace the Unemployment Assistance Act.[1] Although it did not replace the Blind Persons Act and the Disabled Persons Act, it gave the provinces a vehicle for consolidating these categorical programs into a single assistance program. Provinces could also combine the various cost-shared categorical programs with their own assistance programs to create a totally integrated system. Agreements under Part I of CAP had to meet certain conditions. In order to establish national standards, provinces had to agree not to require a period of residency as a condition of eligibility. Use of a needs-test was compulsory, and provinces were required to implement appeal procedures.[2]

---

1 The Unemployment Assistance Act is still in effect in Quebec, Alberta, and the Northwest Territories.
2 Provisions were also made for exchange of statistical information. The federal government was required to carry out occasional administrative reviews and annual financial audits and, upon provincial request, to provide consultative services related to social welfare programs.

Part II of the Canada Assistance Plan contained arrangements under which the federal government could, with the consent of the Indian band involved, make special contributions to provinces agreeing to extend their welfare programs to cover status Indians on reservations or living in Indian communities. Cost-sharing was by special formula to reflect both the federal government's statutory obligation to Indians registered under the Indian Act and the fact that provinces which assumed this responsibility would incur higher expenditures for welfare. Federal-provincial agreements under this section of the act required participation by the Department of Indian and Northern Affairs.

Part III of CAP dealt with special work-activity projects designed to help people who, for environmental, personal, or family reasons, have difficulty obtaining or holding employment. Projects providing technical or vocational training or rehabilitative work-oriented experience were cost-sharable. Importantly, a province could not deny assistance, as covered under Part I of CAP, to persons who refused to take part in a work-activity project.

A summary of the Canada Assistance Plan is presented in Table 1.

The arrangements covering federal contributions to provincial[3] assistance programs clearly indicated CAP's emphasis on needs-testing. Unlike the earlier, categorical programs, which focused upon cause of need (old age, blindness, disabilities, or unemployment), CAP required only that a recipient need assistance. Thus, following the precedent established by the 1956 Unemployment Assistance Act, potential recipients were distinguished on the basis of a needs-test, and any individual judged in need on the basis of such a test, whether employed or not, could become eligible, at the election of the province, for cost-shared assistance.[4]

The application of a needs-test to the population at large potentially expanded the scope of assistance to include the working poor. More significantly, the needs-test introduced the possibility of higher rates of assistance,

3 In Newfoundland, Prince Edward Island, and New Brunswick, all assistance is administered by the provincial authority (Canada Year Book 1979, 257). In all other provinces, both the province and municipalities provide assistance. In these situations, the municipalities typically assume responsibility only for persons whose needs are 'short-term'. Regardless of local arrangements, CAP agreements involve only the two senior levels of government.

4 The act defines a 'person in need' as '(a) a person who, by reason of inability to obtain employment, loss of the principal family provider, illness, disability, age or other cause of any kind acceptable to the provincial authority, is found to be unable (on the basis of a test established by the provincial authority that takes into account that person's budgetary requirements and the income and resources available to him to meet such requirements) to provide for himself, or for himself and his dependents or any of them, or (b) a person under the age of twenty-one years who is in the care or custody or under the control or supervision of a child welfare authority, or a person who is a foster-child. ...'

TABLE 1
Summary of the Canada Assistance Plan

Part I

General assistance

eligibility: needs test

federal cost-sharing: 50 per cent of all costs.

coverage: basic requirements (food, shelter, clothing, utilities, household supplies, and personal requirements); prescribed special needs; care in homes for special care; travel and transportation; funerals and burials; health care services; prescribed welfare services (rehabilitation, casework counselling, assessment, referral, homemaker, and daycare services); comfort allowances and other prescribed needs of residents or patients in hospitals or other prescribed institutions.

Welfare services

eligibility: needs test or likelihood of need if services not provided.

federal cost-sharing: 50 per cent of increased costs of welfare services after 1964–65 fiscal year.

coverage: rehabilitation; casework; counselling, assessment and referral services; adoption; homemaker, daycare, and community development services; administration, consulting, and research services.

Part II—Indian welfare

Special provisions to provinces which extend welfare programs covered in Part I or any part thereof to Indians registered under the Indian Act.

Part III—Work-activity projects

eligibility: needs test; difficulty finding or holding a job.

federal cost-sharing: 50 per cent of costs.

coverage: approved projects designed to provide work-oriented experience.

---

since account could be taken of any gap between individuals' or families' budgetary requirements and their incomes and resources. This was in contrast to the earlier, means-tested programs, under which assistance was based only on income and resources and limited by income and benefit ceilings. Because budgetary requirements were defined very broadly under CAP, provinces were left with considerable leeway in establishing their own needs-tests and in fixing levels of assistance.

The variety of assistance measures cost-sharable reflected CAP's strong rehabilitative emphasis. Shareable costs included not only those incurred to meet the basic material needs of recipients (referred to in the act as 'basic requirements' and defined to include food, shelter, clothing, utilities, household supplies, and personal requirements), but also most costs associated with items required to satisfy the 'special needs' of a recipient. Special items covered ranged from tools or equipment necessary to carry on a trade or find employment to special food, clothing, or appliances required by disabled recipients.[5] Rehabilitation services purchased on a fee-for-service basis were also sharable.

The cost-sharing provisions under general assistance extended to other areas as well. CAP provided for federal sharing of the cost of maintaining needy persons in homes for special care, such as homes for the aged, nursing homes, hostels for transients, homes for unmarried mothers, and child welfare institutions. Provisions were also made to share expenses associated with special health care services not covered under the Hospital Insurance and Diagnostic Services Act or the Medical Care Act, particularly optical, dental, and pharmaceutical services. Finally, the Plan extended coverage to include both costs associated with the care of children under the control or supervision of child welfare authorities and the funeral and burial costs of persons who, at the time of death, were considered in need. Under CAP, then, the federal government reimbursed each province for 50 per cent of the costs incurred by the province and its municipalities when providing assistance, in any form outlined above, to persons in need. Only capital costs were not sharable. Federal contributions were open-ended.

Eligible sharable costs for social services included all costs incurred by provincially approved welfare agencies. Thus, in addition to welfare services supplied directly by provinces and their municipalities, services supplied by voluntary agencies receiving provincial or municipal funds were also eligible. For example, over 350 voluntary agencies (including children's aid societies, family welfare bureaus, etc.) were recognized for cost-sharing purposes under the Plan in 1970–71 (CAP Annual Report, 1970–71, 10).

IMPLEMENTATION AND OPERATION OF THE CANADA ASSISTANCE PLAN

By August 21, 1967, all the provinces except Quebec had entered into direct cost-sharing agreements with the federal government under Part I of the Plan, which deals with general assistance and welfare services. Quebec took advantage of the opting-out provisions of the Established Programs (Interim Arrangements) Act and elected to receive a four-point income tax abatement in lieu of conditional grants. However, although 'the flow of funds to Quebec is chan-

---

5 Expenditures for special need required federal approval only if the cost of an item exceeded $500.

nelled differently through tax arrangements and payments from the Department of Finance, the province presents its claims to the Department of National Health and Welfare and carries out the same provisions in the cost-sharing agreements as do all the other provinces' (Splane 1977, 218).

To date no province has entered into agreements under Part II of the Plan. As a consequence, the provision of Indian welfare has occurred through other channels. Indians, like other Canadians, are entitled to receive benefits through the federal social security system (automatically in the case of universal programs such as Family Allowance, Old Age Security Pensions, and the Guaranteed Income Supplement, and subject to the standard qualifying requirements in the case of social insurance schemes such as the Canada/Quebec Pension Plans and Unemployment Insurance). Unlike other Canadians, however, Indians are not necessarily entitled to benefits from provincial assistance programs. To deal with this anomaly, which arises because Indian affairs fall within federal jurisdiction while social assistance falls within the domain of the provinces, special federal-provincial agreements have been signed (the most important being the 1965 Agreement with Ontario). Alternatively, direct assistance programs have been established through the Department of Indian and Northern Affairs.[6]

All ten provinces have been party to agreements under Part III of the Plan, which deals with work-activity projects. Each work-activity project is the result of a separate federal-provincial negotiation. In any year certain provinces may have no projects in place, although in some years as many as 56 projects affecting over two thousand persons have been in operation across Canada (CAP Annual Report, 1974–75, 5).

With the signing of agreements under Part I, it became possible to pursue the Plan's basic objective: the development of an integrated, comprehensive general assistance program aimed at Canadians in need. Consequently, provinces were encouraged to cease accepting new applications for old age assistance and for blind and disabled persons' allowances and to begin assisting the aged, the blind, and the disabled through their general assistance programs. The transfer to general assistance of recipients under these categorical programs was also encouraged.

---

6 There are also two main categorical income maintenance programs for war veterans: War Veterans Disability Pensions and War Veterans Allowance. Federal responsibility in this area is based upon its constitutional authority for 'Militia, Military and Naval Service, and Defence' under S.92(7) of the BNA Act. Provinces have not sought jurisdiction for this group, although when the proposed Canada Assistance Plan was being debated in Parliament in 1966 it was suggested that an amendment to the War Veterans Allowances Act be included. The suggestion was not accepted.

Between 1966 and 1970, many of the provinces ceased accepting applications under the categorical programs. In 1966, Saskatchewan consolidated its categorical programs into the Saskatchewan Assistance Plan. In 1967, Ontario developed the Family Benefits Program and both Newfoundland and Prince Edward Island transferred their old age assistance and disabled persons programs to a general assistance program. A year later, Alberta consolidated its programs and Nova Scotia ceased accepting applications under its disabled persons allowance program. In 1970, Quebec transferred its categorical programs to general social assistance, and during the seventies the remaining provinces adopted similar policies.

Meanwhile, the federal government carried out its own withdrawal from the cost-shared categorical programs. First affected was the Old Age Assistance program, which shared with the provinces the cost of assistance payments to persons over 65. This program was phased out indirectly as the age of eligibility under the Old Age Security Act was lowered from 70 to 65 by one year of age each year starting in 1966. By 1970, all applicants under the Old Age Assistance program were now eligible for pensions under the Old Age Security Act. Over the same period, the blind and disabled persons allowance programs were also wound down. Provinces signing on with CAP were required to give notice of an intention to include the blind and disabled under CAP (the notice period was 'negotiated'), or a province could give comparable benefits under its own assistance programs. The programs finally expired on February 1, 1981.

The operations of the Canada Assistance Plan may be indicated by summarizing expenditure trends and numbers of recipients. Table 2 indicates the expenditure growth associated with the Canada Assistance Plan and its impact on expenditure originating from the categorical programs. Over the period 1967–77, total cost-shared expenditure under the Canada Assistance Plan grew substantially, from just under $700 million to over $3.1 billion. Over the same period, expenditures for the Old Age Assistance, Allowances for Blind Persons, Allowances for Disabled Persons, and Unemployment Assistance programs experienced a dramatic decline – from a peak of $407 million in 1967 to $1.4 million in 1978.

The shift from the categorical programs to the Canada Assistance Plan is also evident in Table 3, which illustrates the changes in actual coverage by number of recipients within the various programs. Note that both Tables 2 and 3 indicate the success of the Canada Assistance Plan as a vehicle for integrating a variety of independent programs. As well, both tables indicate the expansion in coverage and the growth in cost-shared expenditures which accompanied the introduction of CAP.

Table 4 shows the changing relationship between federal expenditure and gross national expenditure (GNE). Although total federal expenditure and

TABLE 2
Federal-provincial cost-shared expenditure by program ($ thousands)

Year	Allowances for Blind Persons Program	Old Age Assistance Program	Allowances for Disabled Persons Progam	Unemploy- ment Assistance Program	Total categorical expenditure	Canada Assistance Plan
1962	8,260	61,622	32,867	175,798	278,549	—
1963	9,764	76,358	39,269	192,948	318,339	—
1964	9,976	78,416	40,413	214,740	343,545	—
1965	11,249	90,018	46,731	215,106	363,104	—
1966	10,947	85,842	47,602	203,414	347,805	—
1967	10,210	63,980	47,124	286,542	407,847	685,422
1968	7,921	36,000	30,713	88,140	162,774	783,732
1969	7,198	13,282	28,680	33,564	82,724	900,258
1970	6,603	1,688	23,790	29,280	61,361	1,194,864
1971	5,720	—	19,418	28,258	53,396	1,454,754
1972	3,925	—	8,580	2,148	14,653	1,536,460
1973	3,448	—	7,588	2,676	13,712	1,649,550
1974	2,713	—	5,378	1,288	9,379	2,112,138
1975	2,069	—	3,483	126	5,678	2,758,930
1976	1,471	—	2,258	1,283	5,012	3,204,302
1977	1,194	—	1,040	126	2,360	3,123,562
1978	742	—	736	—	1,478	3,367,568

SOURCES: Health and Welfare Canada (1979, 29–35); Canada Assistance Plan, Annual Reports (various years).

federal expenditure through the Canada Assistance Plan have both been increasing as a percentage of GNE, expenditure through CAP remains relatively insignificant – less than 1 per cent of GNE and less than 4 per cent of total federal expenditure. Table 5 illustrates the significance of Canada Assistance Plan expenditure relative to total social security outlays. It can be seen that CAP expenditure in 1980–81 amounted to less than 10 per cent of total federal spending on social security.

Table 6 presents a disaggregation by several components of federal expenditure under the Canada Assistance Plan. Although payments toward general assistance clearly represent the most significant aspect of the Plan, it is interesting to note that the other parts of the Plan account for almost 40 per cent of total CAP expenditure.

TABLE 3
Federal-provincial cost-shared assistance programs, numbers of recipients

Year	Blind Persons Program	Old Age Assistance Program	Disabled Persons Progam	Unemployment Assistance Program	Total categorical expenditure ($)	Canada Assistance Plan ($)
1962	8,573	98,944	50,029	684,348	841,894	—
1963	8,634	103,159	50,621	760,466	922,880	—
1964	8,581	105,241	51,671	727,961	893,454	—
1965	8,586	107,354	53,106	717,030	886,076	—
1966	8,149	84,959	54,191	789,694	936,993	—
1967	7,582	58,363	53,863	—	119,808	—
1968	5,808	24,922	34,438	—	64,168	1,336,471
1969	5,267	6,147	30,663	—	42,077	1,346,009
1970	4,818	4,818	25,739	—	35,375	1,622,071
1971	4,015	—	18,608	—	22,623	1,533,295
1972	2,916	—	9,468	—	12,384	1,369,985
1973	2,557	—	8,213	—	10,770	1,347,376
1974	1,814	—	4,369	—	6,183	1,436,010
1975	1,560	—	3,902	—	5,462	1,491,408
1976	1,002	—	1,566	—	2,568	1,508,400
1977	886	—	1,274	—	2,160	1,501,914
1978	806	—	1,080	—	1,886	1,547,579

SOURCES: Health and Welfare Canada (1979, 29–35); Canada Assistance Plan Annual Reports (various years).

THE SHORTCOMINGS OF CAP

The Canada Assistance Plan is an attempt by the Government of Canada to use its spending powers to encourage the development of better social assistance and social service programs. The federal promoters of CAP may be said to have had two fundamental goals in mind:

1. The creation of a reasonably consistent national welfare apparatus, and
2. An extension of assistance to anyone who might need it – need being the only criterion.

However, because responsibility for social programs resides with the provinces, and because of certain inherent shortcomings in the CAP legislation itself, these goals remain elusive.

TABLE 4
Federal government expenditure trends, separated by program type

Year	GNE	Government expenditure (federal) (millions of dollars)				Expressed as a % of GNE		
		Excluding transfers	Including transfers	CAP	Categorical programs	Including transfers	CAP %	Categorical programs
1962	42,927	6,352	7,486	—	139.275	17.4	—	0.325
1963	45,978	6,440	7,609	—	159.166	16.5	—	0.346
1964	50,280	6,758	8,010	—	171.773	15.9	—	0.342
1965	55,364	7,120	8,551	—	181.552	15.4	—	0.328
1966	61,828	8,089	9,753	—	173.903	15.8	—	0.281
1967	66,409	8,998	10,990	342.711	203.924	16.5	0.516	0.307
1968	72,586	9,857	12,229	391.866	81.387	16.8	0.545	0.112
1969	79,815	10,743	13,465	450.129	41.362	16.9	0.564	0.052
1970	85,685	11,865	15,262	597.432	30.681	17.8	0.697	0.036
1971	94,450	13,063	17,386	727.377	26.700	18.4	0.770	0.009
1972	105,234	15,568	20,126	768.230	7.335	19.1	0.730	0.006
1973	123,560	17,625	22,422	824.775	6.858	18.1	0.667	0.005
1974	147,528	22,704	28,869	1,056.069	4.689	19.6	0.716	0.004
1975	166,343	27,838	35,508	1,379.465	2.839	21.5	0.829	0.002
1976	191,031	30,182	38,704	1,602.151	2.506	20.3	0.839	0.001
1977	208,806	33,840	43,807	1,561.781	1.180	21.0	0.748	0.001
1978	229,698	38,089	48,974	1,683.784	0.739	21.3	0.733	0.000

SOURCES: Canadian Tax Foundation (1981, 23–30); Health and Welfare Canada (1979, 29–35); Canada Assistance Plan Annual Reports (various years).

TABLE 5
Federal government social security expenditure, 1980–81

Function or expenditure source	($ millions)	Percentage of total social security expenditure
Old Age Security	7,383.0	38.0
Family Allowances	1,852.0	9.54
CANADA ASSISTANCE PLAN	1,857.3	9.57
Vocational rehabilitation	49.1	0.253
New Horizons	11.8	0.061
Welfare grants	6.4	0.033
Categorical programs	.4	0.000
National Health & Welfare—administration	62.1	0.320
Unemployment Insurance	4,621.9	23.810
Canada Pension Plan	2,023.4	10.425
Department of Veteran Affairs	1,006.4	5.185
Department of Indian Affairs	471.2	2.427
Department of Justice	26.9	0.138
Department of Labour	17.5	0.090
Department of Social Development	3.4	0.009
Other	19.6	0.075
Total	19,407.3	

SOURCE: Canadian Tax Foundation (1981, 121).

TABLE 6
Federal expenditure under CAP, various components ($ thousands)

Year	General assistance	Homes for special care	Child welfare	Health care	Welfare services	Work activity	Total
1968	260,950	61,417	21,417	25,514	22,540	27	391,865
1969	290,135	46,476	57,253	24,909	31,336	19	450,129
1970	391,066	103,510	40,334	22,128	40,353	41	597,432
1971	493,574	132,586	41,235	11,869	47,514	599	727,377
1972	513,603	141,638	44,715	10,789	56,404	1,081	768,230
1973	539,693	138,600	56,200	10,700	77,300	2,282	824,775
1974	687,425	182,049	62,231	22,795	98,508	3,601	1,056,069
1975	803,439	324,352	62,432	25,915	149,359	3,968	1,379,465
1976	904,165	421,264	67,617	32,405	171,813	4,887	1,602,151
1977	993,300	259,295	75,757	30,005	200,260	3,165	1,561,781
1978	1,089,498	247,523	82,431	33,217	228,287	2,828	1,683,784

NOTE: Figures are rounded.
SOURCE: Canada Assistance Plan Annual Reports (various years).

TABLE 7
Comparison of provincial social assistance programs

Province	Eligibility	Services covered	Assistance levels
Newfoundland	—Needs test	—Assistance to needy —Child care services —Homes for special care	$ 7,200
Prince Edward Island	—Budget deficit system	—Assistance to needy —Homes for the aged —Child care services —Limited number of homes and sheltered workshops for those in need	6,900
Nova Scotia	—Budget deficit system	—Assistance to needy —Child welfare services —Homes for the aged and disabled	6,400
New Brunswick	—Needs test	—Assistance to needy —Child welfare services —Special care homes —Rehabilitation of disabled persons	6,700
Quebec	—Budget deficit system	—Assistance to needy —Institutional care —Child welfare services	7,200
Ontario	—Needs test for the provincial benefits plan, which is designed primarily for long-term needs —Budget deficit method for the municipally administered general welfare assistance plan, which is primarily for short-term needs	—Assistance to needy —Homemakers and nurses services —Homes for the aged —Vocational rehabilitation services —Family counselling —Child welfare services —Mental retardation —Community services	6,900
Manitoba	—Needs test	—Assistance to needy —Homes for the elderly and infirm —Child welfare services	8,000

TABLE 7 continued

Province	Eligibility	Services covered	Assistance levels
Saskatchewan	—Needs test	—Assistance to needy —Senior citizens benefits —Homes for the aged —Child welfare services —Rehabilitation counselling, community development, etc.	6,700
Alberta	—Needs test —Single unemployed employables receive benefits only up to 31 days	—Assistance to needy —Senior citizen benefits —Homes for aged —Child welfare services	10,500
British Columbia	—Needs test	—Assistance to needy —Services to handicapped and aged —Child welfare services	9,100

NOTE: Assistance levels are based on the level of assistance available to a family of four with 'average needs', plus provincial and federal family allowances and the child tax credit (calculations based on 1980 data).
SOURCES: Boadway and Kitchen (1980, 234–36); Ross, D. (1981, 58).

The CAP legislation specifies that eligibility for assistance under programs cost-shared through CAP must be determined on the basis of a needs test. However, it is left to the provinces to define 'need' and to set levels of assistance. CAP can only provide broad and flexible guidelines to the provinces, which establish their own programs on the basis of local and regional circumstances (particularly community and cultural norms, the incidence of poverty, and the availability of resources). Given the regional diversity of a federal state the size of Canada, and given the flexibility of CAP, the scope and quality of assistance programs necessarily varies widely across provinces. Table 7 presents a summary of the various provincial assistance programs, illustrating key differences in eligibility, services covered, and assistance levels.

The diversity of provincial programs and the existence of considerable regional disparity has had a significant impact on actual program operation. Table 7 indicates that assistance levels vary widely across provinces – reflecting, in part, differences in provincial tax capacity and, in part, differences in provincial tolerance of inequality. The dependency rate (recipients as a percentage of population) varies significantly as well. This can be seen from Table 8, which shows that dependency rates in 1977–78 ranged from 9.6 per cent in New Brunswick to 3.6 per cent in Saskatchewan. It would appear that this variation reflects economic conditions (particularly per capita incomes and unemployment rates) rather than the generosity of the various programs (see Table 7). Table 8 also reveals the importance of women as recipients of social assistance. In 1977–78, 58 per cent of all social assistance cases in Canada involved families with female heads of households.

Provincial autonomy with respect to social programs seriously undermines several of CAP's major objectives. The Plan's aim has been to develop a system that would emphasize the right to benefits, raise levels of assistance, broaden coverage, and help the unemployed reenter and remain in the work force. But provincial programs have generally maintained a categorical approach (frequently classifying recipients as employable or unemployable to separate classes of beneficiaries for different treatment), established maximum levels of assistance, and denied access to the working poor.

The provinces' failure to establish the right to assistance was identified in the White Paper on Income Security (Canada 1970, 53).

A fundamental weakness in the administration of social assistance in Canada is the failure to recognize that persons unable to support themselves have a right to assistance. ... Judgements of whether a person is 'deserving' or not still enter into decisions about eligibility and the amount of assistance. People are often denied assistance even when the alternative options of employment, training or rehabilitation are not really available.

CAP has done little to abate the punitive use of eligibility conditions – citizens who, for reasons beyond their control, require assistance continue to be stigmatized. Moreover, provinces frequently fail to let applicants know exactly where they stand under the law – a failure which leaves potential recipients unclear as to when they are entitled to assistance (Guest 1980, 157–58).

The right to appeal, built into all CAP agreements and offering recipients recourse to administrative decisions, has failed to materialize to any appreciable extent. Appeal boards, where established, too often act as extensions of provincial welfare departments. Information available to applicants and recipients about their right to appeal is limited. Moreover, little effort is made to publicize the decisions of appeal tribunals. Although the provinces made substantial

TABLE 8
Social assistance recipients by province, 1977–78

Province	Average monthly number of recipients	Recipients as a % of population: dependency rate	Male heads of households: number and % of cases	Female heads of households: number and % of cases
Newfoundland	49,649	8.8	9,433 (50%)	9,431 (50%)
P.E.I.	6,847	5.7	1,400 (43%)	1,872 (57%)
Nova Scotia	49,616	6.0	8,410 (40%)	13,208 (60%)
New Brunswick	65,776	9.6	12,331 (44%)	15,693 (56%)
Quebec	456,944	7.2	108,189 (45%)	134,775 (55%)
Ontario	353,949	4.2	66,210 (38%)	106,128 (62%)
Manitoba	47,954	4.8	9,190 (40%)	13,784 (60%)
Saskatchewan	34,360	3.6	6,111 (39%)	9,233 (61%)
Alberta	82,919	4.3	12,123 (34%)	23,729 (66%)
British Columbia	139,410	5.6	22,722 (42%)	31,378 (58%)
Total	1,292,127	5.6	257,226 (42%)	359,940 (58%)

NOTE: 'Recipients' includes dependents while 'cases' covers the family unit.
SOURCES: Canadian Intergovernmental Conference Secretariat (1980, 145–46)

TABLE 9
Comparison of social assistance levels and poverty lines for a family of four, 1980[a]

| Province | Social assistance[b] | Statistics Canada poverty lines | | Canadian Council on Social Development poverty line[d] |
		Population over 500,000[c]	Population over 30,000[c]	
Newfoundland	$ 7,200	$12,870	$10,780	$13,530
P.E.I.	6,900	12,870	10,780	13,530
Nova Scotia	6,400	12,870	10,780	13,530
New Brunswick	6,700	12,870	10,780	13,530
Quebec	7,200	12,870	10,780	13,530
Ontario	6,900	12,870	10,780	13,530
Manitoba	8,000	12,870	10,780	13,530
Saskatchewan	6,700	12,870	10,780	13,530
Alberta	10,500	12,870	10,780	13,530
British Columbia	9,100	12,870	10,780	13,530

NOTES: a Change in all items Consumer Price Index for 1980 was 10.29 per cent.
b See note to Table 7.
c Statistics Canada poverty lines for a family of four adjusted by size of residence (estimated for 1980 by adjusting for changes in all items C.P.I.)
d The Canadian Council on Social Development (CCSD) poverty line based upon one half of average Canadian family income (estimated for 1980 by adjusting for changes in all items C.P.I.)
SOURCES: Ross (1981, 58); Canada. Dept. of Finance (1981, 164).

efforts to improve appeal procedures during the 1970s, lack of information continues to be a major weakness in the Canadian public assistance system.

Assistance levels have remained low in spite of CAP. Generally, provision is made only for the most essential items, and in some provinces assistance is further limited by fixed ceilings on payments set without consideration of actual needs or costs. With continuing inflation, the absence of statutory provisions for indexing in all but two provinces (Nova Scotia and Quebec) has further compounded problems associated with inadequate assistance.

Assistance is even more inadequate in those provinces retaining a categorical approach. Unemployed employables are often eligible for aid only on an emergency basis. In many cases, emergency aid covers only food, leaving recipients without access to other essential items, such as clothing and shelter. Social assistance levels, presented in Table 7, are compared with three poverty-line measures in Table 9. By all standards of comparison, assistance levels must be judged inadequate.

CAP's stipulation of 'need or likelihood of need' as the only criterion for eligibility for assistance under the Plan was hailed as a major innovation. In practice, however, most provinces are unwilling to assist families with working members, even though many of these households are in need as need is defined by the Plan. Thus, a significant portion of the Canadian poor are denied access to public assistance. Yet CAP's failure in this regard is not entirely the fault of the provinces. Several provinces have in fact introduced income supplementation programs that extend benefits to the working poor (see Chapter 5). However, because these programs dispense assistance largely on the basis of income rather than tested need, they are denied eligibility under CAP – a circumstance that limits their efficacy and discourages other provinces from experimenting with similar programs. Thus the 'need or likelihood of need' provision of the CAP legislation, quite contrary to its intent, has itself proved to be an obstacle to a solution to the problem of poverty in Canada.

4
Federal structure and redistribution: a theoretical framework

This chapter sketches a framework for examining redistributive policy in a federal state. Because conventional economic analyses of federalism concentrate on issues of allocative efficiency, few guides are available for examining questions of redistribution. The following analysis takes a social welfare approach and focuses directly on the well-being of individuals, interpreting redistribution alternatively in anti-poverty and in egalitarian terms. Our aim here is to provide a context for examining federal-provincial social policy; discussion of technical details is left to the appendices.

POVERTY MEASURES AND REDISTRIBUTION

How much should the government transfer to those 'in need'? To what extent should 'equalization of incomes' be pursued? What tax rate would be required to finance a given level of redistribution? These are fundamental policy questions. A first step to addressing them is to discuss the measurement of poverty.

The simplest measure of poverty or income-need is the proportion of persons in a society whose income is below some predetermined poverty line, x^*. Because this ratio ignores the degree to which those who are poor fall short of the poverty line, the sum total of all shortfalls from x^* is often used as an alternative poverty measure. This 'poverty gap' is the aggregate dollar amount necessary to eliminate poverty. However, the poverty gap does not indicate the relative ease or difficulty with which a society can eliminate poverty.

Another index, $P(x^*)$, relates the poverty gap to the total income of a society. The measure $P(x^*)$ is the percentage of total income that must be transferred from the non-poor to the poor in order to raise the income of everyone below the poverty line to x^*. It may also be viewed as the average tax rate required to finance the elimination of poverty. If x* is set at the average income level of society, P(x*) then becomes the percentage of total income that must be transferred to equalize incomes. In other words, anti-poverty objectives, in the sense of transferring sufficient income so that all individuals have at least x* income, and egalitarian objectives, in the sense of equalizing incomes, shade into one another from the perspective of the index P(x*). The poverty index P(x*) may therefore be viewed more generally as a transfer or redistributive index. Society's social objective may be characterized as the provision of basic support if x* is less than the average income for society. Alternatively, society's philosophy is egalitarian if x* is established as the average income for society.

In a federal state, the population can be assigned to mutually exclusive regions called provinces. The measure P(x*) can be defined for each province or for the country as a whole. The proportion of poor in the country will be a weighted average of the proportion of poor in each province, the weights being proportional to the population of each province. Similarly, the mean income of the poor in the country will be a weighted average of the mean income of the poor in each province, the weights being proportional to the income share of the poor in each province. Finally, the poverty index of the country will be equal to a weighted average of the poverty indexes in each province, the weights being proportional to the income share of each province. (See Appendix A.)

This proposition suggests how a federal, decentralized government structure can decompose a national redistributive objective into provincial elements. Obviously, the amount of redistribution or anti-poverty effort depends upon the level chosen for x*. A high poverty line involves more redistribution and therefore requires a higher average tax rate than a low one. Moreover, x* need not be identical for all provinces. Each province could establish its own poverty level, in which case there would not be national uniformity. Again, each province might have a different fixed transfer amount or maximum implied tax rate, in which case the amount of redistribution or anti-poverty effort would vary by province. The relevant conclusion is that a nationally established redistributive objective can be specified and decomposed into provincial components for analysis or policy implementation; alternatively, provincial efforts may be aggregated to assess overall national performance.

INCOME INEQUALITY AMONG THE POOR

The poverty index P(x*) is defective from a social welfare perspective because it ignores income inequality among the poor. To correct this deficiency, some adjustment factor is necessary. The Gini index is commonly used to measure income inequality.[1] It is possible to calculate the Gini index (G*) for incomes below x* and to incorporate this measure to obtain poverty indexes which are sensitive to the degree of inequality among the poor, mean income remaining unchanged. We may then consider the elasticity of the poverty index with respect to inequality; that is, the percentage reduction in the poverty index if incomes among the poor were redistributed so as to reduce G* by 1 per cent. The elasticity relates the effect of income inequality among those with incomes below x* to the poverty index. Two alternative poverty indexes incorporating G* are calculated for Canada and the provinces later in this chapter. Both measures, P_1 and P_2, have an elasticity less than unity, meaning that if incomes among the poor were redistributed to reduce G* by 1 per cent, the poverty measure would be reduced by less than 1 per cent. The elasticity of P_2 is less than that of P_1; consequently P_1 is more sensitive than P_2 to changes in income inequality among the poor. Thus, if greater importance is attached to inequality of income among the poor, P_1 is preferable to P_2. (Further details are provided in Appendix A.)

NEGATIVE INCOME TAX MECHANISMS AND POVERTY

There are many ways to transfer income to the poor. One general mechanism is the negative income tax or guaranteed income. Income transfer schemes can be analyzed in terms of the components of guaranteed income or negative tax plans. Virtually all income maintenance proposals contain a basic support level, S, for which units are eligible if they have no income, and some rate of 'offset' or taxation, B, by which the support level is reduced for each dollar of income. Consequently, a guaranteed income plan is often characterized by its combination of the guaranteed minimum support, S, and its offset taxation rate, B; x* can thus be redefined as that level of income at which transfers or payments are no longer given. For a constant taxation rate, B, this 'breakeven' level is equal to S/B. The higher the minimum guarantee and/or the lower the tax rate, the higher is the break-even level and, consequently, the greater the proportion of the

---

1 The Gini index is formally defined as half the absolute mean difference in incomes between each pair of individuals, relative to mean income. The index is easier to visualize by considering the Lorenz curve, which plots on the horizontal axis the percentage of total income received by each poorest x per cent of the population. If income were equally distributed, the Lorenz curve would be a straight line representing the hypotenuse of the triangle whose sides are the horizontal and vertical axes. When income is not distributed equally, the Lorenz curve lies within this triangle. The Gini index is then the area bounded by the Lorenz curve and the hypotenuse divided by the total area of the triangle. The Gini index has a value between zero and one. Consult Kakwani (1980) for a formal treatment of Lorenz curves and the Gini index.

population receiving payments. It is also convenient to depict a guaranteed income plan as a negative tax. Viewing x^* as a tax 'threshold' level of income, a negative income tax plan operates as follows. Units with incomes exceeding x^* are taxed at a fixed B per cent on the excess; units with incomes below x^* are granted transfer payments (negative taxes), again at a fixed rate of B per cent on income below x^*. Given only the mild restriction that the threshold level of income exceed the mean income of the poor, the mean income of the poor is always raised by a negative tax plan. Furthermore, a negative tax plan will result in a more equal distribution of income overall. Because negative tax plans produce these results, it is worth noting the essential principle underlying the negative tax model – namely, income-testing. The basic idea is the scaling of benefits inversely to income level: the lower the income, the higher the benefit (negative tax).

ALTERNATIVE DEFINITIONS OF THE TARGET THRESHOLD

There is much controversy surrounding the choice of x^*, hereafter called the target threshold. This section outlines alternative definitions of the target threshold and relates them to different social welfare philosophies and institutional situations.

ABSOLUTE POVERTY LINE. The target threshold is frequently defined as some absolute number of dollars or some basic level of services. This interpretation adopts an anti-poverty objective, with poverty or need defined in absolute terms. The Statistics Canada (Revised 1973) poverty line is based upon an absolute or subsistence approach. The intended recipient units are people.

RELATIVE POVERTY LINE. The target threshold is defined in terms of some fraction of the average (or median) income in society. This interpretation also sees redistribution in terms of anti-poverty objectives, but defines poverty in relative terms. The approach of the Canadian Council on Social Development (1979, 5) is based upon a relative concept of poverty; the Council suggests that the poverty line be set at one-half of the average Canadian income. The intended recipient units are people.

INCOME EGALITARIANISM. The target threshold is defined as the average level of income in society. This interpretation views redistributive objectives in an egalitarian spirit, since its aim is to equalize incomes (individual or group means). The intended recipients may be people or groups (provinces).

INCOME-TEST AND GUARANTEE. The target level is viewed as the break-even level in a guaranteed income plan with basic support, S, and subsidy rate, B. This interpretation views redistribution in terms of providing a basic guarantee but scaling further transfers inversely to additional income. Intended recipients may be people or provinces.

EQUALIZATION. The target level is defined in excess of the average of the collectivity. For example, it might be set at the mean income of the highest (or n highest) of the provincial mean incomes. This is neither pure redistribution nor income-sharing; it entails injection of net funds for distribution. Within the context of provincial revenue-sharing schemes, a net transfer of funds from the federal government is necessary. Provinces are typically the recipients of central government transfers.

To summarize, the definition of the target threshold is crucial; it serves to distinguish among such redistributive objectives as: eliminating poverty, guaranteeing basic minima, or equalizing incomes. The context of the redistribution – whether it be among individuals or between levels of government – is also important.

FISCAL INCIDENCE AND THE POWER TO REDISTRIBUTE

The level of x^* may denote either public goods or 'specific goods' – that is, goods or services produced by government but otherwise similar to private goods in the sense of being consumed exclusively by their 'owner'. Many goods have both a 'public good' component and a 'specific good' component (Weisbrod 1964). For example, goods such as medical care, unemployment insurance, or social and rehabilitative services have three analytically separate dimensions: a collective consumption option-demand component, an individual consumption component, and an equal need component (Gillespie 1980, 79–80). An individual may expect unemployment insurance benefits sometime in the future; he is therefore prepared to 'pay' for this option. Since the provision of this option to one individual does not preclude its being equally available to everyone else, this is the classic Samuelsonian case of a public good. At the same time, individuals may receive specific services or benefits (e.g., a medical operation, private counselling, or unemployment insurance payments). These specific goods are clearly similar to private goods. Finally, concern over the limited or constrained level of consumption of certain goods (e.g., medical services) by low-income individuals often justifies public spending that delivers basic universal benefits on the assumption that all have equal need for the good (Lindsay 1969).

There is no difficulty, then, in interpreting the target threshold level x* in terms of public or mixed goods, whether x* be an absolute basic level of services, a level of services equal to the national average, or a level equal to some fraction of the national average. The basic service may be guaranteed to those with no income whatever and thereafter adjusted by income or user charges. The level of public goods may also vary by province, and attempts to ensure uniformity by equalization among provinces may or may not imply more than purely redistributive philosophies.

The above in no way minimizes the difficulty of determining the fiscal incidence of public or mixed goods. Rather than inquiring into the proportion of taxation burdens borne by various income classes or provincial groupings (tax incidence) or imputing the value of public goods to various households (benefit incidence), fiscal incidence combines both to 'measure ... the change in relative income positions of ... units, grouped by size classes of income, in response to the taxation and public expenditure policies of the public sector. The term "fiscal incidence" refers to the extent to which the public sector redistributes income. ...' (Gillespie 1980, 8). Some social evaluation function of alternative income distributions is all that is required to complement studies of fiscal incidence for a social welfare approach.

A fundamental question in a federal state concerns the allotment of the redistributive power, since the ability to affect the distribution of income or well-being of individual citizens determines overall social welfare. Should the power to redistribute be given to the federal or to the provincial governments? Or shared?

The general view is that the redistributive power should be assigned primarily to the central level of government (Musgrave 1959), although a case can be made to the contrary (Breton and Scott 1978). In Canada, recent debate has highlighted the importance of national standards and the question of whether the amount of redistribution is greater or less with a particular assignment (West and Winer 1980 a, b; Usher 1978, 1980 a, b). Given provincial diversity in social and economic affairs under highly decentralized government, West and Winer argue for 'a reduced emphasis on maintaining national standards in such areas as health, education, social welfare, ... and so on' (1980a, 9–10). Any requirement for uniformity is countered by an appeal to competition, so what is really at issue is the trust and confidence one places in the disciplinary force of provincial competition.

Usher suggests that 'there would be less redistribution in total under provincial than under federal jurisdiction', and that concurrent assignment of powers fosters disharmony (1980a, 19–20). The essence of Usher's argument involves matching the extent of the tax-transfer group or collectivity with the jurisdictional range (functional responsibility) of the government. Harmony (disharmony) is a positive (negative) externality of government redistributive activity;

consequently the optimal assignment of the redistributive power is to that level of government which can best internalize the externalities. Since Usher's argument is a reflection of the more general debate concerning the optimal assignment of government responsibilities in a federal state, the basic concern may be rephrased as: do we want national redistribution? or merely provincial redistribution? Or, in current rhetoric, is Canada one single community or a bunch of communities?

POVERTY INDEXES FOR CANADA AND THE PROVINCES

Poverty indexes for Canada and the individual provinces are presented below in Tables 10 and 11. Table 10 gives the mean family income and Gini index for each province. It also indicates the average income (u^*) of families with incomes below the target threshold (x^*), as well as the Gini index (G^*) associated with the distribution of incomes below x^*. Three poverty indexes are given: $P(x^*)$, which does not take income inequality among the poor into account; and $P_1(x^*)$ and $P_2(x^*)$, which do. Since the value of any poverty index depends upon the threshold x^*, four alternative definitions of x^* have been selected to represent a range of values. The first definition is $u_i/2$, which is one-half the individual province's mean income. The second definition is $u/2$, which is one-half the overall Canadian mean income. The third definition is simply the Canadian mean income, u. The fourth definition is the maximum value of all the provincial mean incomes.[2]

Table 10 illustrates the extent to which the poverty indexes increase as the target threshold is raised. It also reveals that poverty indexes (P_1 and P_2) which

2 The data are from Statistics Canada, *Income Distributions by Size in Canada*, 1977. Computations similar to those reported in Table 10 for individuals and for families and unattached individuals reveal the same pattern; they are not reported here but are available from the author on request.

 Data on the distribution of personal incomes are typically only provided in grouped form; that is, the total number of persons, or percentage of total persons, falling within different (often broad) income ranges are simply listed. In order to compute poverty indexes and measures of inequality for any arbitrary level of x^*, a general interpolation procedure was employed. The method is from Kakwani (1980) and involves using a separate, continuous differentiable function which fits the data points exactly within each income range. Different functional forms are tried and the 'best fit' form used. In particular, we represent the Lorenz curve by a third degree polynomial within each income class, except the first and last open-ended classes. The first and last income classes are fitted with Pareto curves. Parameters of the income density function are then derived from the fitted curve, and poverty and income inequality measures such as G^* computed for any given value of x^*.

TABLE 10
Poverty indexes by province for family units, 1977

Province	Mean income	Gini	u*	P(x*)	$P_1(x^*)$	$P_2(x^*)$	G*	x*
Nfld.	16456	.318	6201	.0315	.0468	.0447	.158	$u_i/2$
			7223	.0614	.0891	.0849	.176	u/2
			11626	.3715	.5012	.4749	.254	u
			12167	.4393	.5851	.5553	.257	max u_i
P.E.I.	16050	.305	5442	.0325	.0458	.0436	.195	
			6648	.0627	.0876	.0834	.203	
			11599	.3793	.5066	.4815	.246	
			12198	.4485	.5943	.5651	.251	
N.S.	16505	.313	5643	.0340	.0483	.0460	.194	
			6692	.0610	.0853	.0812	.200	
			11507	.3632	.4848	.4605	.250	
			12056	.4248	.5662	.5383	.254	
N.B.	16888	.315	5526	.0373	.0526	.0499	.217	
			6425	.0599	.0834	.0791	.221	
			11579	.3455	.4636	.4399	.252	
			12168	.4084	.5429	.5155	.255	
Quebec	19056	.295	6226	.0352	.0492	.0468	.211	
			6473	.0410	.0567	.0539	.212	
			12397	.2430	.3384	.3197	.244	
			13110	.2925	.4024	.3809	.243	
Ontario	21600	.277	6750	.0344	.0478	.0452	.234	$u_i/2$
			6378	.0283	.0399	.0377	.236	u/2
			13133	.1646	.2391	.2247	.240	u
			13907	.2020	.2874	.2712	.234	max u_i
Man.	18421	.308	5679	.0416	.0581	.0548	.246	
			6071	.0520	.0715	.0677	.245	
			12007	.2729	.3797	.3574	.264	
			12623	.3254	.4455	.4205	.263	
Sask.	17960	.319	5673	.0421	.0584	.0554	.225	
			6285	.0559	.0776	.0735	.232	
			11720	.3013	.4121	.3890	.263	
			12286	.3569	.4813	.4553	.264	
Alberta	21251	.290	6460	.0410	.0572	.0539	.256	
			6160	.0355	.0501	.0471	.259	
			12142	.1850	.2606	.2446	.268	
			12981	.2217	.3095	.2912	.263	
B.C.	21040	.286	6136	.0413	.0565	.0534	.262	
			5935	.0370	.0510	.0481	.262	
			12188	.1852	.2617	.2455	.268	
			13097	.2223	.3122	.2935	.262	

TABLE 11
Poverty indexes for Canada, alternative units, 1977

(I) *Unit = families*

Mean Income	Gini	u*	P(x*)	$P_1(x*)$	$P_2(x*)$	G*	X*
20101	.293	6354	.0376	.0525	.0497	.232	u/2
		12472	.2118	.2988	.2814	.251	u
		13219	.2555	.3555	.3356	.248	max u_i

Weighted index P(x*) x* =	$u_i/2$	u/2	u	max u_i
	.0364	.0376	.2132	.2570

(II) *Unit = individuals*

9747	.439	2359	.0921	.1214	.1140	.338	
		4302	.3270	.4235	.3973	.373	
		4583	.3703	.4792	.4494	.377	

Weighted index P(x*) x* =	$u_i/2$	u/2	u	max u_i
	.0909	.0923	.3277	.3710

(III) *Unit = families & unattached individuals*

16764	.303	3447	.0500	.0605	.0581	.300	
		6056	.2155	.2535	.2445	.312	
		6252	.2550	.2942	.2854	.290	

Weighted index P(x*) x* =	$u_i/2$	u/2	u	max u_i
	.0629	.0645	.2684	.3109

take into account income inequality among the poor have larger values than P(x*); that P_1 is more sensitive to income inequality than P_2; and that there is variation across provinces in all these measures as well as in the mean income and degree of income inequality (G*) among the poor.

Table 11 presents similar information for Canada, employing as alternative definitions of the income-receiving unit: the family, the individual, and families and unattached individuals. A weighted index for Canada is also calculated for the four alternative definitions of x* listed above.

CONCLUSION

A number of important conceptual issues are raised by our social welfare approach to federalism and redistribution. Is society's aim the elimination of poverty among individuals? Among provincial aggregates? Is its objective to equalize individual incomes? or provincial mean incomes? Should there be more or less decentralization of the redistributive power? Should federalism be viewed as a matter of multi-tiered governments, each level responding to individuals? or in terms of power relations between the levels of government themselves?

Despite apparently wide differences in institutional details, the theme of redistribution recurs in discussions of social policy. Our aim has been to provide a general framework for examining social policy in a federal-provincial context. Issues raised by the Canada Assistance Plan differ only in degree and detail from considerations normally associated with Established Programs Financing and Equalization.

5
The Canada Assistance Plan and the working poor

In 1979, over two and one-half million Canadians lived in poverty.[1] Of greater significance is the fact that approximately 55 per cent of poor families were headed by individuals in the labour force. This group is often referred to as the 'working poor'. The working poor typically do not receive income assistance, since the Canadian social assistance system assumes a clear dichotomy between those who cannot or should not work (the aged, the blind, the disabled, women with small children, etc.) and those deemed able-bodied and, therefore, employable. Those capable of employment are expected to meet their needs through their own efforts; consequently, only the unemployable have been considered worthy of public support.

The employable-unemployable dichotomy had become entrenched in Canadian policy thinking by the early 1950s. The employable were to be assured income adequacy by minimum wage legislation. Fiscal and monetary policy would maintain full employment, and unemployment insurance would give protection against the risk of unemployment. On the other hand, the unemployable – the aged, the blind, and the disabled – would receive support through federally cost-shared provincial programs. Aid for the residual 'unemployed but employable' group that did not qualify for unemployment insurance remained a joint responsibility of municipalities and provinces (CIGS 1980, 15). However, in 1956 the Unemployment Assistance Act extended cost-sharing to provincial programs providing assistance to this group. Despite this patchwork of programs, the fundamental problem for the working poor remained – inadequate income.

1 This estimate is based upon the Statistics Canada revised low-income cut-offs. The cut-offs take into account family size and size of area of residence and are designed on the basis of 1969 Family Expenditure Survey data. Cut-offs refer to income levels such that family units spend, on average, 63 per cent or more of their income on food, shelter, and clothing.

The consolidation and extension of federal cost-sharing and the introduction of a 'needs test' under the Canada Assistance Plan were potentially significant for the working poor. The sole requirement under CAP was that a person be 'in need'; for the first time, therefore, provincial assistance to those working but also 'in need' became cost-sharable. However, although provincial programs for income supplementation exist, they are generally independent of assistance programs cost-shared under CAP; this is due in part to the manner in which the CAP legislation is set out. Furthermore, although the Social Security Review intended to replace CAP with an income support and supplementation scheme, several provinces rejected the proposal. The failure of the Review not only left the working poor in most provinces without an income supplementation program: it also jeopardized the income supplementation programs developed by some provinces in anticipation of new cost-sharing arrangements.

Existing provincial policies have not solved the problems of the working poor. Minimum wage rates remain low and fail to take into account the family responsibilities of the worker.[2] Table 12 compares minimum wage income with social assistance payments. While there is substantial variation across provinces, only in Quebec does minimum-wage income significantly exceed the social assistance payment level for households with children. Moreover, social assistance levels are invariably adjusted for family size: in all provinces, the income advantage of social assistance *vis-à-vis* minimum wage grows larger as the number of children present increases.

Even when the various income supplementation schemes are taken into account, the income of low (and minimum) wage workers remains below the poverty line (see Table 13). In any case, not all provinces have supplementation schemes. Low wage workers in any of the Atlantic Provinces, for example, are without provincial supplementation. Provincial welfare programs in all but four provinces (Quebec, Ontario, Nova Scotia, and Saskatchewan) contain substantial work disincentives, since minimum wage earners (heads of a family of four)

---

2 This is not to suggest that an increased minimum wage would be an appropriate policy instrument for eliminating poverty among the working poor. Most low-income workers actually earn more than the current minimum wage. Very large increases in minimum wage rates would be required to move most families out of poverty (National Council of Welfare, 1981, 90–105). Moreover, minimum wage legislation may only exacerbate unemployment problems and lead to other undesirable effects (see West and McKee 1980). Also, the correlation between low wages and low family income may not be as strong as is generally presumed (Simpson 1981).

TABLE 12

Net minimum wage income as a percentage of social assistance income by province and family size, 1980.

	Nfld	PEI	NS	NB	Que	Ont	Man	Sask	Alta	BC
One adult	143	125	120	152	177	174	153	164	155	145
Two adults	93	98	91	101	128	109	112	119	102	101
One parent, one child	88	91	88	95	132	102	105	104	103	89
One parent, two children	83	79	74	91	121	90	89	87	86	76
One parent, three children	80	72	67	88	116	81	79	83	78	68
Couple, one child	89	85	77	95	120	97	94	98	87	85
Couple, two children	85	78	70	92	114	88	84	92	79	76
Couple, three children	83	71	64	89	111	81	76	87	74	71

NOTE: Minimum wages are net employment related expenses and (for single parent families) child care costs to allow a more realistic comparison than if gross minimum wage incomes were used.
SOURCES: National Council of Welfare (1981), 101.

would be better off drawing social assistance (see Table 13). Instead of ameliorating the lot of the working poor, provincial policy tends in many cases to penalize them for working.

This chapter examines income maintenance for the working poor within the context of the Canada Assistance Plan provisions. It considers the policy trade-off in delivering income transfers to the working poor and comments on provincial responses in income supplementation.

INCOME TRANSFERS TO THE WORKING POOR – MAJOR
POLICY ISSUES

This section analyses the formal relationship between program design (tax rate schedule, tagging, etc.) and policy trade-offs (costs of program, adequacy of benefits, etc.) within the generic framework of the negative income tax (NIT) mechanism. Every income transfer program may be characterized succinctly in terms of the standard parameters of the NIT, namely the basic support level or 'guarantee', S, and the benefit reduction rate (offset rate), B. A break-even point is given by S/B; the break-even point is that income level at which cash transfers or 'negative taxes' are no longer paid.

TABLE 13

Comparison of minimum wage, supplemented incomes, and social assistance expressed as a percentage of the Statistics Canada poverty lines for a family of four, 1979–80[a]

	Annual minimum wage income	Supplemented annual income[b]	Social assistance
Newfoundland	53.2[c]	59.7	66.1
	(59.2)[d]	(66.3)	(74.1)
Prince Edward Island	(58.6)[d]	(65.3)	(70.5)
Nova Scotia	52.4[c]	58.8	58.8
	(58.2)	(65.3)	(65.3)
New Brunswick	53.2[c]	59.7	61.5
	(59.2)	(66.3)	(68.4)
Quebec	61.9[e]	77.4	61.9
	(73.5)	(91.8)	(73.5)
Ontario	53.3[e]	61.9	59.3
	(63.3)	(73.5)	(70.5)
Manitoba	54.2[e]	64.5	68.8
	(64.3)	(76.5)	(81.6)
Saskatchewan	67.1[c]	80.8	61.5
	(74.5)	(89.8)	(68.4)
Alberta	53.3[e]	60.2	90.3
	(63.3)	(71.4)	(107.1)
British Columbia	53.3[e]	60.2	78.3
	(63.3)	(71.4)	(92.9)

NOTES: a Adapted from Ross (1981, 58).

b Supplemented annual income is the net cash supplement available from all sources in 1979 at the particular annual minimum wage income (benefits minus taxes and premiums).

c Poverty line adjusted for size of largest provincial urban centre—population 100,000 – 499,000.

d Poverty line for centres with population less than 30,000.

e Poverty line adjusted for size of largest provincial urban centre—population over 50,000.

SOURCES: Annual minimum wage income, supplemented incomes, and social assistance are from Ross (1981, 58). Poverty lines are from Statistics Canada, Income Distributions by Size, 1979, 20.

The higher the support level (S) and/or the lower the offset tax rate (B), the higher will be the break-even point and the larger the proportion of the population receiving cash transfers. Total program costs will also be larger or, equivalently, the average tax rate necessary to finance the program will be higher. High support levels are often advocated on grounds of 'income adequacy'; a given support level is judged to be either unacceptably short of some absolute poverty line or too small a fraction of the average income standard. But high support levels may lead to undesirable effects. For example, income transfers may cause the breakup of families (Bishop 1977); or again, high support levels and low offset rates may discourage work effort.

The fundamental policy conflict between program costs, adequacy of benefits, and incentive structures may be set out more formally. Consider a negative income tax program defined by

$$T = -au + tY, \tag{5.1}$$

where T is 'negative' tax payments and a is the fraction of average per capita income (u) received by a person with zero income; thus au is the basic support level. The marginal rate of taxation on earnings (Y) is represented by t. A slight rearrangement of (5.1) yields the more familiar payment formula identified with a NIT design (Hum 1981b):

$$\begin{aligned} P = -T &= au - tY \\ &= G - tY. \end{aligned} \tag{5.2}$$

Summing (5.1) over all individuals in society and dividing by total income yields

$$\begin{aligned} \Sigma T_i &= \Sigma(-au) + \Sigma tY_i \\ &= -anu + t\Sigma Y_i. \end{aligned}$$

Hence

$$\frac{\Sigma T_i}{\Sigma Y_i} = g = -a + t, \text{ or}$$

$$g = -a + t. \tag{5.3}$$

Equation (5.3) establishes the fundamental policy trade-off (Akerlof 1978). The magnitude g is the ratio of net taxes collected to total income and can be taken as a measure of program costs. Higher levels of support can only be achieved by raising marginal tax rates. The effect of higher marginal tax rates on individual behaviour is usually phrased in terms of work disincentives. The direct cash transfer (au), itself a potential work disincentive, might also engender effects such as family splitting and marital dissolution.

The policy conflict between generosity (a), incentive structures (t), and costs (g) implied by Equation (5.3) reflects the separate concerns of different professional groups. The emphasis of academic economists on the tax structure and labour supply (t) is a measure of their concern with work incentives, productivity, and labour markets. The quest by the social work profession for an 'adequate income' for the poor is typically expressed in attempts to define the 'poverty line' and to argue for increased assistance levels (a). Finally, the overall financial cost to government (g) is often the chief concern of public officials, particularly those in finance and treasury departments. The point remains that a fundamental conflict exists between costs, incentives, and benefits. Whatever the special pleading of any particular group, no program can simultaneously 'not cost too much', 'provide adequate benefits', and 'create no work disincentives'. The virtue of the negative income tax principle lies in its income-testing feature, whereby benefits are scaled inversely to income; it is this basic principle which allows some scope for compromise.

In contrast to the simplicity and elegance of an NIT scheme, present social assistance programs are often fragmented, redundant, complicated, and distorted (CIGS 1980, ch. 4). To a great extent the defects of existing programs derive from what Akerlof (1978) calls 'tagging', by which is meant the use of various characteristics to identify groups for special treatment. As a result of tagging, income transfer programs become 'categorical'. Some categorical programs, called 'demogrants', employ demographic characteristics such as age (Old Age Security) or family status (Family Allowances). Other categorical programs are based on 'subjective' tests such as 'availability for work' (Unemployment Insurance) or 'likelihood of need' (Canada Assistance Plan). In all these cases, income transfers are given to specific categories of people on the basis of assumed need. But whether categorical transfer programs (i.e., tagging) actually reduce poverty depends upon whether the groups singled out for special treatment and the low-income population are in fact one and the same. To the extent that tagging fails to accurately identify the low-income population, it only serves to aggravate the policy conflict implied by Equation 5.3. On the other hand, accurate tagging of the poor would be one means of reducing that conflict.

Suppose the poor comprise a fraction p of the population, and that they can be unambiguously tagged. The poor are given basic support at a level of, say, $S = au$; the non-poor are not given any support. Everyone is subject to a common marginal tax rate t. The set of programs then comprises

$$T_i = -au + tY_i \quad \text{for p, and}$$
$$T_i = o + tY_i \quad \text{for } 1 - p.$$

It is easy to show that tagging results in Equation (5.3) being amended to:[3]

$$g = -pa + t. \tag{5.4}$$

Equation (5.4) reveals that the ability to tag the poor improves the trade-off between g, t, and a. In particular, tagging allows for higher support levels for the poor with less distortion to the tax structure.

Yet tagging may be costly to administer, and it may even induce individuals to alter their characteristics in order to qualify for special treatment. For example, it is commonly alleged that significant numbers of people feign job searches in order to be tagged as 'available for work' and hence eligible for Unemployment Insurance benefits (see Hum 1981a). In terms of an anti-poverty objective, tagging can be justified only if it is relatively cheap to administer, if it will not create opportunities for individuals to alter their condition so as to receive benefits, and if the tagged group and the poor are one and the same. The popularity of demogrants may be due to the relative ease with which they meet the first two of these conditions; however, the last condition is an empirical one and is not generally satisfied by many of the tags frequently used in Canada.

Two other policy designs may be indicated briefly. Suppose the support level G = au is made universal but that the 'poor' are offered a tax rate different from that imposed on the non-poor.[4] In other words, we have:

---

3 See Akerlof (1978) for proof. Below, we present an easier alternative which will prove useful for manipulating other program designs. Since

$$T_i = -au + tY_i \quad \text{for p, and}$$
$$T_i = o + tY_i \quad \text{for (1-p),}$$

hence

$$pT_i = -apu + ptY_i$$
$$(1-p) T_i = \quad + (1-p)tY_i.$$

Therefore

$$\frac{\Sigma T_i}{\Sigma Y_i} = \frac{-pa\Sigma u}{\Sigma Y_i} + \frac{t\Sigma zy_i}{\Sigma Y_i}$$
$$g = -pa + t,$$

which is (5.4).

4 For example, this could be a universal, taxable demogrant in conjunction with a progressive income tax system. It is not always the case that the non-poor face a lower marginal tax rate. Because of the phenomenon of 'tax stacking', the poor may face marginal tax rates that exceed those faced by higher income groups. It is sufficient for our purposes that the tax rates faced by the two groups be simply different.

$$T_i = -au + t_1 Y_i \quad \text{for p, and}$$
$$T_i = -au + t_2 Y_i \quad \text{for } 1 - p.$$

It is easy to show[5] that the fundamental trade-off becomes:

$$g = -a + [p\ t_1 + (1 - p)\ t_2]. \tag{5.5}$$

Finally, the Castonguay-Nepveu Report proposed two support levels and two tax rates (Quebec 1971). For those not expected to work, a high support level and high tax rate was suggested. For those with a significant attachment to the labour force and some potential for additional work-related income, a second plan with a lower support level and lower tax rate was contemplated. The scheme can be represented algebraically as

$$T_i = -a_1 u + t_1 Y_i \quad \text{Plan One for q population, and}$$
$$T_i = -a_2 u + t_2 Y_i \quad \text{Plan Two for } 1 - q \text{ population.}$$

It is again fairly easy to show that the Castonguay-Nepveu two-part plan is a weighted average of two NIT programs:

$$g = [-qa_1 - (1 - q)a_2] + [qt_1 + (1 - q)t_2]. \tag{5.6}$$

Table 14 summarizes the major policy trade-offs associated with different program designs. It is evident that categorical programs (tagging) affect the policy trade-off through a, while giving the poor a different marginal tax rate (which we term income-testing)[6] affects the trade-off through the structure of the tax schedule. The Castonguay-Nepveu plan is a combination of tagging (work/ no work distinction) and income-testing (two tax rates). The notion of adequate support levels (a_i) is also determined by tags in this proposal.

The foregoing discussion suggests important policy questions. Should income assistance be delivered on a categorical or tagging basis? Or should the

---

5 *Supra* note 3. The same technique is used: multiply each program equation by its appropriate population proportion, add, and divide by total income. The equation which follows next in the text (5.6) is derived in similar fashion.

6 Income-testing has a dual interpretation. It may refer to the netting out of taxes in the payment of transfers or, alternatively, it may refer to a divergence of marginal tax rates. See Kesselman and Garfinkel (1978, 181).

TABLE 14
Summary of policy trade-offs and income transfer program designs

Program design	Trade-off
Standard NIT	$g = -a + t$
Guarantee by TAG to poor only	$g = -pa + t$
Universal guarantee,	
different tax rate to poor	$g = -a + [pt_1 - (1-p)t_2]$
Two guarantees, two tax rates	
(Castonguay-Nepveu Plan)	$g = [-qa_1 - (1-q)a_2] +$
	$[qt_1 + (1-q)t_2]$

DEFINITIONS: g = ratio of net taxes to total income
a = fraction of average per capita income employed to establish
    guaranteed support level
t = marginal tax rate on earnings
p = proportion of population "tagged"
q = proportion of population eligible for support component of
    two-tier plans

transfer system focus upon the income-testing principle? Despite the heated debate over categorical versus income-tested programs, the general superiority of
one transfer method over another cannot be established. Non-categorical income-tested transfers can reduce poverty to a greater extent than categorical programs if the tagged groups do not correspond closely to the low-income population. On the other hand, tagging may create less distortion in the incentive
structure; it may also select those in special need very efficiently (as in the case of
manpower programs and social services).[7] In short, the policy gains of any redistribution must be weighed against the losses due to adverse incentive effects
(Akerlof 1978, 13).

There are other, more narrow policy questions. Should the 'working poor' be
treated as a separate group? Could a sufficiently discriminating tag be
found? Would the working poor require a specially designed delivery system?
Because every tag implies a social (or political) judgment concerning the 'worthi-
ness' of the group receiving income transfers, the question of whether the
working poor should receive special attention is controversial, the focus of the

7 Manpower programs and social services illustrate the added dimension of in-kind transfers
rather than income transfers. In many instances services may be tied to income. CAP per-
mits the use of tags to identify special needs for calculation of the amount of the income
transfer.

controversy being the work-disincentive effects that such attention would allegedly bring.

The policy interest surrounding this controversy is easy to understand. The greater the reduction in work effort, the larger is the cost of income maintenance for the working poor. Further, because society expects the able-bodied to work, any work-disincentive effect attributed to income transfers erodes public support for assistance programs. Worry over the possible work-disincentive effect of income transfers has led policy makers to retain the basic distinction between the working poor and all others who are poor. For example, discussion of possible guaranteed income designs retains the notion of a separate support level for the working poor (e.g., the Castonguay-Nepveu proposal), who are to be distinguished (tagged) from the general population on the basis of various 'employment-availability' or 'work-eligibility tests (Social Security Review Proposal, Communiqué, June 1–2, 1976). In sum, the work-disincentive issue would seem to provide a *prima facie* basis for retaining a very important categorical distinction in income maintenance.

The magnitude of any labour-supply reduction is an empirical matter. The importance of reliable estimates of labour-supply withdrawal has occasioned five large-scale social experiments in negative income taxation – four in the United States and one in Canada (Hum 1980a). The results from the American experiments are the best prime source of information about the probable work-disincentive effect of income transfers to the working poor. The estimated withdrawals differed in each experiment – and differed significantly by demographic group – ranging from 2.5 per cent to as high as 20 per cent (Hum 1980b)[8]. Whether these magnitudes are too high to justify a guaranteed income for all is a matter of political judgment. However, the social experiments also reported favourable (and unfavourable) response effects unrelated to work effort. Thus any conclusions drawn about the economy-wide or social effects of a universal income maintenance program should be based on broader considerations than work reduction alone.

The question remains whether or not the working poor should be categorized as a distinct group for income maintenance and, if so, how this categorization should be achieved. Society is willing to provide income transfers to the population in need, but at the same time it insists upon its members' reciprocal obligation to contribute to their support according to their capacity; thus the

---

8 See Hum (1980b) for a description of the experiments and their design as well as for a survey of the work disincentive findings. The experimental results vary widely and have not been subject to much scrutiny by professionals. Basilevsky and Hum provide a critical evaluation in a forthcoming volume to be published by Academic Press, New York.

issue of work disincentive is likely to recommend continued categorization. But categorization may be less objectionable and administratively cumbersome if 'self-categorization' is adopted. Rather than relying upon subjective assessments of eligibility such as 'likelihood of need', an income maintenance strategy designed to include the working poor might consider wage subsidy or earning supplementation mechanisms. The exact details and administrative advantages of such schemes are not of concern here (see Kesselman 1969, 1973 for a discussion); the important point is that such designs minimize work disincentives by confining transfers to those who work positive hours.

The major limitation of the current CAP arrangements remains the fact that despite CAP's avowed attempt to abandon the traditional categorical approach, a categorical approach with respect to the working poor persists. However, the problem is not categorization *per se*, but rather the inequity of rewarding some of those in 'need or likelihood of need' and not others. 'If *all* categories were to be rewarded, but on different conditions, then the incentives for individuals to falsify their true traits would be reduced. Further, the magnitudes of inequity ... would be lessened'. (Kesselman 1973, 67.) Some categorization scheme to segregate the working poor from those who cannot or should not work is probably necessary. What is unsatisfactory is to exclude the working poor altogether. But despite CAP's attempt to extend assistance to all of 'those in need or likelihood of need', the working poor have generally been excluded from provincial income maintenance programs.

THE PROVINCES AND INCOME SUPPLEMENTATION

Only three provinces – Saskatchewan, Quebec, and Manitoba – have implemented general income maintenance programs which apply to the working poor (see Table 15). The Saskatchewan Family Income Plan (FIP) was the first such program. FIP, which provides monthly payments to families with dependent children, was introduced in 1974 as a transitional program to be merged eventually with whatever income supplementation scheme resulted from the Social Security Review (Ross 1981, 51). When no such scheme emerged, Saskatchewan was forced to seek funding for FIP under CAP, but since cost-sharing under CAP is contingent on needs-testing, not all expenditures under FIP were sharable. As a consequence, eligibility conditions were tightened (Saskatchewan Information Services 1976) and benefit levels were allowed to decline, while political support for the program lessened (Riches 1978). In the case of FIP, the needs-test requirement of the Canada Assistance Plan proved to be a major stumbling block.

TABLE 15
Summary of income-tested supplementation programs

Income-tested direct transfer programs	Date of implementation	Jurisdiction	Cost-sharing	Details
Saskatchewan Family Income Plan	1974	Provincial	Limited cost-sharing under CAP	Maximum benefit of $50 per month per child for first three children; $40 a month for each additional child. If after-tax income <$6,200, the maximum benefit is payable. Payments reduced by $0.50 for every dollar of income above the limit for maximum benefits.
Quebec Work Income Supplementation Plan	1979	Provincial	None	Applicants complete a special form with their provincial income tax returns and submit it to the Quebec Department of Revenue, which determines eligibility and amount of benefits. The program assures that families and individuals are financially better off working than on welfare. Those earning less than or equal to what they would receive under social assistance can apply for an income supplement equal to 25 per cent of the earnings. Maximum benefits go to those earning incomes equal to the social assistance level. Benefits are reduced by one dollar for every three dollars of earnings above the social assistance level.
Manitoba Child Related Income Support Program	1981	Provincial	None	Maximum benefits of $30 a month per child. If total family income (including federal family allowances and child tax credits) adjusted by $500 per child <$7,500, the maximum benefit is payable. Benefits reduced by $0.25 for every dollar of income above the maximum.

SOURCE: National Council of Welfare (1981), 105–20.

Nonetheless, the Family Income Plan was an important development. As an income-tested program, FIP incorporated a tax-back rate of less than 100 per cent; thus, in contrast to other social assistance programs, FIP provided substantial work incentives.[9] The Saskatchewan program also set a significant precedent by establishing provincial jurisdiction over a supplementation program of this type, thereby assuring some measure of integration with provincial social assistance schemes.

Only Manitoba and Quebec have followed Saskatchewan's lead and established fairly general income-tested programs providing direct cash payments to poor families. Quebec introduced its Work Income Supplementation Program in 1979 specifically to aid the working poor (see Tamagno 1979 for a description). The Quebec Plan operates as a supplement to earned income and is self-categorizing. Only those who work and have low earnings relative to their overall family needs receive income supplements. The supplements decline as income increases, and the program is designed to complement other income security programs, such as Family Allowances and minimum wage laws. Thus the Quebec program represents a significant advance in income maintenance for the working poor.

The Manitoba program is called the Child Related Income Support Program (CRISP) and was introduced in 1981. (See Hum and Stevens 1980 for an analysis.) As its name suggests, the program is child-related in terms of determining eligibility. Since the program delivers cash supplements on the basis of income rather than earnings, it is not specific to the working poor, although it includes those working poor with children. CRISP was introduced by the Conservative government, but the New Democratic Party assumed office in the program's initial year of operation and has established a task force to review social assistance. Consequently, the fate of CRISP and the future direction of income maintenance policy in Manitoba are uncertain. At present, the program is not cost-shared under CAP.

It is important to note the very special circumstances which led the three provinces with income supplementation programs to introduce them. Saskatchewan introduced its plan in order to establish a claim over jurisdiction and in anticipation of new cost-sharing arrangements. It also wanted to integrate its

9 Although earnings from work do not decrease assistance payments dollar-for-dollar (100 per cent tax back), financial work incentives are quite limited. In most provinces, full-time earnings are either sheltered up to some fixed amount (with earned income above this level being taxed back at a high, usually 100 per cent, rate) or a fixed percentage of earned income (gross or net) is exempted. The FIP offers greater work incentives because payments are reduced by only $0.50 for every dollar earned above a specified income level. For a description of FIP, see Saskatchewan, Department of Social Services (1976).

program with the Saskatchewan Assistance Plan. Quebec has a long history of harmonizing its social programs, and its introduction of a program for the working poor reflects its ongoing resolve to develop an independent and comprehensive social security system specific to its provincial needs. Manitoba, arguably, showed interest in introducing the CRISP reforms only when the Conservative government faced an election and feared that its earlier and severe restraint policies would be too well remembered. But since the initiatives of Saskatchewan, Quebec, and Manitoba can be ascribed to exceptional circumstances, the question remains of why the provinces have, in general, not responded to the needs of the working poor.

Part of the explanation must be the nature of the cost-sharing arrangements under CAP, in particular the requirement of a needs-test. This requirement forced Saskatchewan to concede changes in the design of its program in order to obtain limited federal funding. The Quebec and Manitoba programs do not use needs-tests; consequently neither program is eligible for cost-sharing. In other words, the 'need or likelihood of need' provision of the CAP Act has proved costly to those few provinces with income supplementation programs aimed at the working poor. The present CAP legislation is therefore a considerable obstacle to the development of income maintenance programs for the working poor in other provinces.

CAP was an attempt to decategorize income maintenance. Yet categorical programs continue to be the favoured delivery design, not only for the purpose of limiting costs but also as a means of extending assistance explicitly to those groups commanding wide sympathy. Thus, both the provinces and the federal government have made great strides in programs aimed at the elderly, a group favoured by the public. On the other hand, neither level of government wants to embark on income maintenance for the working poor, since such programs would be costly and not particularly popular. The working poor have yet to conjure up as sympathetic an image in the public mind as, say, the pensioner.

CONCLUSION

The condition of the working poor may well grow worse. Increases in the minimum wage have not kept pace with inflation since 1975 (National Council of Welfare [1981], 104). Furthermore, unemployment remains high and eligibility for Unemployment Insurance benefits has been tightened. The introduction of separate federal and provincial income supplementation and tax credit schemes has intensified problems of coordination. As provinces initiate programs in response to local pressures and demands, program stacking may occur, affecting tax rates and making integration of different programs difficult. Moreover, provinces have become increasingly vulnerable to unilateral federal initiatives; reductions in federal program outlays (as with Unemployment Insurance) may increase provincial assistance expenditures. Cooperation between levels of government has been affected and is perhaps now at an all-time low. The need for a coordinated income supplementation scheme is greater today than ever, yet the obstacles to such a scheme – the problems of income adequacy, program cost, work incentives, and jurisdictional responsibility – remain unresolved.

The Canada Assistance Plan sought to shift the focus of transfers from groups of 'deserving poor' to all 'in need or likelihood of need'. But the issue of the 'working poor' has never been satisfactorily addressed. This failure has been due in part to the divided and unsettled allocation of responsibility for the working poor, and in part to government's anxiousness to preserve work incentives among this group. Yet a share of the blame must go to the 'need or likelihood of need' provision of CAP itself, which inhibits the extension of cost-sharing to programs for the working poor. At a minimum, the CAP legislation should be revised to allow the use of income-testing in place of needs-testing.

6
The Canada Assistance Plan and social services

Social services in Canada have developed under both private and public auspices. At the time of Confederation, social services were provided largely by voluntary and religious organizations. Although provinces and municipalities were constitutionally responsible for social service provision, they were reluctant to expand their severely limited involvement in this field. However, as awareness of the social consequences of poverty increased during the 1960s, public support for increased public provision began to grow.

In response to new demands and regional disparity in the level and quality of services, the federal government decided to take the initiative.[1] Three pieces of legislation, the Medical Care Act, the Hospital Insurance and Diagnostic Services Act, and the Canada Assistance Plan Act – all introduced in 1966 – changed the face of Canadian social policy. Now, government commitment to social welfare also included the provision of social services.

The term social services, which this study has used indiscriminately so far, requires clarification.[2] Social services include the complete range of provisions

1 Bella (1979) has argued that in the case of the Canada Assistance Plan it was provincial social welfare initiatives rather than federal initiatives that were paramount. Federal policy was merely designed to accommodate provincial desires and innovations, particularly those of Alberta (in the case of preventive social services) and Ontario (in the case of child welfare).
2 Attempting an authoritative definition for social services is a waste of time. Some countries include income maintenance, health programs, education, public housing, and employment programs among social services. Recent British literature refers to 'personal social services' as the 'fifth social service' to distinguish it from education, health, housing, and income maintenance. Kahn (1979, 19) would add non-market employment programs as a 'sixth service'. Even a definition of 'personal social services' includes such disparate activities as day care, homemaker services, family guidance, child welfare, juvenile guidance and correction, family planning, community centres, nutrition programs, therapeutic work activity,

which promote the health, education, and well-being of individuals and communities. Even a restricted definition would include the numerous manpower, health care, and education programs which have become so comprehensive in Canada as to achieve independent institutional identity.[3] Medical care and education are accorded separate treatment in federal-provincial cost-sharing under the Established Programs Financing Act. The remaining social services are commonly described as 'human services' or 'personal social services', of which 'welfare services' comprise a sub-group. It is 'welfare services' which are covered under the Canada Assistance Plan.

The Canada Assistance Plan commits the federal government to paying one-half of any increase in provincial expenditure on welfare services. Eligibility for cost-sharing is limited to those services having as their main objective 'the lessening, removal, or prevention of the causes and effects of poverty, child neglect, and dependence on public assistance' (CAP Act 1966, 4). Eligible services include services related to rehabilitation; casework, counselling, assessment, and referral services; adoption services; day care and homemaker services; and community development services. Services related wholly or mainly to education, correction, or recreation are not covered, nor are any health care services within the meaning of the Hospital Insurance and Diagnostic Services Act.

Access to services under CAP is limited to the 'poor' population. It was originally intended that the Plan would cover a larger population, in the hope that service provision might prevent poverty. However, this broader approach did not materialize in the legislation, and access to welfare services was restricted to 'persons in need'. Although a less restrictive 'likelihood-of-need' test was developed, the take-up rate among non-assistance recipients was low. Welfare services received the same stigma as the assistance programs; people stayed away to avoid being labelled in 'need' or 'on welfare' (Armitage, 1979, 149). Some

---

rural welfare, special group assistance, institutional care, drug abuse, etc. (see Kahn 1979, 12–13 for a more complete listing). Among Canadian writers, Armitage (1979, Ch. 7) prefers the term 'personal and community social services'; specifically, he distinguishes four types: social utility services (e.g., day care, family planning, information services), social adaptation services (e.g. child welfare and parental abuse), institutional resource services (e.g., nursing homes), and community adaptation services (e.g., community development services). See also Hepworth (1975) for specific services. The CAP Act uses the term 'welfare services'.

3 For an interesting historical hypothesis as to how education and health services obtained independent institutional identity, see Kahn (1979, 21–24).

provinces, notably Alberta, developed special preventive social services programs to overcome this problem.[4]

By the early 1970s, pressure to reform CAP had developed. The restrictions on access to services were considered objectionable. To many, it seemed unreasonable to deny an individual access to a needed service simply because he was not poor according to the CAP regulations. Provinces therefore began to show interest in new areas of social service provision and felt their policy choices were being distorted by CAP (Heagle 1978, 102).

For policy analysts, the events of the last decade pose many problems. Particularly troublesome is the lack of consensus about the place of social services in public policy. Should social services simply 'rehabilitate' the poor by assisting their participation in the labour market; that is, be the handmaiden of employment policy? Or should they be considered part of the 'new property rights' of every citizen?

This chapter isolates certain policy issues associated with services covered under the Canada Assistance Plan. However some issues are relevant to social services in general. The framework of Chapter 4, with its emphasis on fighting poverty and the reduction of inequality, is employed as a basis for discussion. At the outset, it is important to note that the social welfare approach does not necessarily imply a commitment to public provision of social services. If social services are seen as private goods, then direct cash transfers coupled with provision through the marketplace could well be the most efficient route. On the other hand, social services might be more appropriately viewed as either mixed or public goods, in which case the issues surrounding income redistribution and those concerning social service provision are intrinsically different. This is the view adopted here.

PERSONAL SOCIAL SERVICES – THE ISSUES

CAP was designed to function as an integral part of Canada's anti-poverty program. Essential to that program is the view that poverty is the result of

---

4 Opinions differ concerning whether Alberta's preventive social services legislation was developed in anticipation of CAP cost-sharing, or whether the design of CAP evolved in response to Alberta's influence. Bella (1979, 440–41, 446–47) takes the latter view. Bella's quotation of Alberta welfare minister Halmrast's letter to federal Health Minister La Marsh (*Ibid.*, 446) might be interpreted either way. In any event, when technical decisions over 'phrasing' led federal officials to adopt the term 'likely to be in need' to describe the conditions for cost-sharing, portions of Alberta's preventive social services program became eligible (*Ibid.*, 447).

individual defects in either aspiration or ability, a view given expression in economic theory in terms of human capital deficiencies. Human capital refers to that bundle of skills, abilities, motivations, and attitudes which a person offers to the labour market. The larger the amount of human capital possessed, the greater the productivity and hence the higher the wage rate commanded. On the other hand, those with insufficient human capital are destined for poverty. Consequently, government provision of social services for the purposes of increasing an individual's human capital (say, through rehabilitation) or by removing individual problems (say, through counselling) represents prudent and sound investment. Social services expenditure is therefore a social investment to combat poverty.[5]

How has this thinking shaped policy toward social services under CAP? The implicit position has been that a poor individual is poor because a particular attribute or personal problem stands in the way of his ability to function adequately in society. As a consequence, the CAP strategy emphasizes problem-solving, or what Kahn (1979) calls 'case services' – the equivalent, from a social work perspective, of the human capital perspective of the economist. It follows that the primary emphasis under CAP is given to services that offer potential returns: rehabilitation services, counselling, assessment and referral, casework, and day care. These services presumably help assistance recipients break the cycle of poverty – a result that yields dividends in the form of individual self support, higher national output, and lower assistance payments. Ironically, social services covered under CAP do not focus on skill upgrading, education, job preparation, or job placement, where, perhaps, the potential returns are highest. The element of social investment strategy in the services provided under CAP is in fact minimal and merely 'remedial'. Consequently, social services under CAP do not receive the degree of support that manpower programs enjoy.

Investment thinking has also shaped the allotment of expenditure among the various services covered under CAP. For example, day care services have not been strongly supported – reflecting the belief of many policy makers that the cost of good day care probably exceeds the expected gains from freeing assistance recipients to work.[6] On the other hand, rehabilitation services, casework,

5 'The ... new element in the [Canada] assistance plan is the support it will provide to the provinces ... for improving and extending social welfare services. ... The aim is to enable assistance recipients to move on to achieve the greatest possible measure of self-support. This is one of the sound and constructive weapons to be used in combating both rural and urban poverty.' (Prime Minister Lester Pearson in House of Commons Debates 1965.)
6 Day care is one of the most topical social services. A recent study by Krashinsky (1977) takes the view that day care subsidies are like wage subsidies. Therefore it is 'inefficient use of public funds' to give day care subsidies amounting to $10,000 to free a mother to earn $6,000 (*Ibid.*, 62).

and counselling enjoy relatively strong support – although even in these areas support tends to be limited relative to the support given to services not under CAP, which promise larger social dividends.

The implicit or explicit use of investment criteria has undoubtedly shaped the social service system that has developed under the influence of the Canada Assistance Plan. Yet upon examination, it is difficult to justify the artificial and restricted conception of 'welfare services' under CAP as simply an anti-poverty strategy. The poor are not the only income group to require family counselling; drug addiction and alcoholism affect people in every income class; and homemaker services might be needed by any family at some time. Thus, the distinction between 'welfare services' (for the poor) and 'personal social services' (for everyone) lies in the fact that the upper- and middle-income classes are served through the marketplace while the poor are served through government support.

Seen in this light, the genus social services is closer to being a benefit-in-kind transfer than a human capital investment. However, the distinction between services as in-kind transfers and services as investments is difficult to maintain in practice, since one can always visualize circumstances in which personal social services do yield returns. Nonetheless, the distinction is necessary. One need look no further than the medical health care system to find a social service with investment potential – yet very few would be willing to justify the provision of health care on the basis of investment criteria. Similarly, the rationale for child welfare services is not that they represent a good investment; rather, provisions for child welfare services reflect basic social values.[7] A child's 'right' to protection and, if need be, support, has actual legal status. Abuse or neglect of children is punishable under the Criminal Code of Canada, and courts have the power to remove any child from a home environment considered unsuitable. As a consequence, many children enter the child welfare system as wards of the court (society), a reflection of broad agreement on social values. The result has been to establish service provision formally in law.

However, few other services enjoy this special status. Is there a case to be made for government involvement in non-statutory service provision? Other questions relevant to personal social services in the broader context of social welfare policy include: Would an optimal system of transfers include both transfers in kind and transfers in cash? Are there criteria for determining the optimal mix? Should only some services be supported and, if so, which ones? Is it appropriate to tag service recipients, i.e., to focus on one particular target

---

7 This special status is also evident in income maintenance policy; for example, Family Allowances, Child Tax Credits, and various provincial income supplementation schemes.

population? Finally, should income redistribution be tied to the service delivery system?

If an investment approach is adopted, most of these questions are easily answered. Service provision would be desirable only when the net present value of the stream of expected returns exceeded the actual cost of providing the service. Investment criteria would simultaneously determine if, and which, services should be provided. *A priori*, the optimal policy would involve tagging, since the distribution of expected returns over the population is likely to be uneven – with expected returns highest among assistance recipients. Finally, a close link between the cash transfer system and the service system would probably be desirable, given the basic purpose of social service provision in an investment framework – namely, to help assistance recipients enter the labour market and support themselves. However, this study takes the view that 'welfare services' under CAP represent in-kind transfers to the poor – rather than an investment in them – and must therefore be addressed in the context of the debate over the efficacy of cash versus in-kind transfers.

Economists have traditionally argued that anti-poverty funds are more effectively allocated when transfers are made through lump-sum cash grants rather than through consumption subsidies or direct provision of goods.[8] Also, social workers claim that providing welfare services may be self-defeating if the poor are offered in-kind transfers, since everyone else uses cash (Kahn 1979, 116). Rather than encouraging self-support (financial or emotional) among the poor, such 'protected' in-kind transfers demonstrate lack of confidence in the poor and perpetuate dependency. Presumably, then, an ideal system would involve only income transfers, with consumer sovereignty and the market being left to allocate resources. However, the alleged superiority of cash over in-kind transfers holds good only under certain conditions: first, the good or service in question must be a pure private good; second, there must be no externalities in consumption (that is, one individual's consumption must not affect the welfare of anyone else); third, donor preferences must be held important, but they must not take the specific form of wanting beneficiaries to consume particular goods and services. Significantly, for most social services these conditions do not hold.

Social services cannot be classified as pure private goods. Although use of a social service by one person reduces the supply available for others (a private

---

8 This is a standard textbook lesson and needs no elaborate reference. The strongest case is usually made in the area of public housing; for example, Aaron and Von Furstenberg (1971) argue that in the United States income transfers could achieve the same housing goals as housing allowances at about 90 per cent of costs. The argument is often too easily transferred to intergovernmental grants, with the predictable result that unconditional grants always make recipient regions better off than other alternatives (e.g., Boadway 1980, 53–54).

good characteristic), it does not preclude the possibility of others using the service in the future. The option to use the service is available to everyone (a public good characteristic), even if it is never used. This option component is important if the market cannot always supply the service when demanded, or if service is of unacceptable quality. Furthermore, private demand might not be sufficient to bring forth the desired supply, in which case the option demand dimension becomes critical.[9] Consider a social service which might be needed only on an emergency basis, such as crisis centres or counselling for victims of crime. Individuals may be willing to pay some price for the option of consuming these services and to assure that services are of high quality. But because no individual can exclude others from consuming the option component of the supplied service, no one will indicate what he is willing to pay to keep the option of consuming open. Thus the service may be under-supplied, if it is supplied at all. In such circumstances, government intervention is necessary.[10]

In the case of some services (crisis intervention services, child welfare services, etc.), the community as a whole does have considerable interest in maintaining high-quality delivery, and support for adequate service provision would be independent of individual use. For other services, particularly those already supplied by the private sector, such as fitness, recreation, or weight loss services, the option demand would not be as significant and in itself would not justify government action. The varied nature of all conceivable personal social services does not permit a definitive statement as to the general significance of the option demand dimension, but this much can be said: the greater the significance of the option demand, the closer the social service lies to the 'mixed' or 'public good' end of the spectrum, and the larger the presumption of need for collective provision.

In a general equilibrium framework, the preferences of both the donor (either government or taxpayer) and the beneficiary must be taken into account. As long as one is willing to argue that the beneficiary's consumption of an actual service (counselling for child abuse, say) is not directly of interest to the donor, the traditional case for cash transfers remains valid. In many cases, however, donors want the beneficiaries to actually consume the service in question. If the consumption externality is present, then the case for in-kind provision on efficiency grounds is strong (Garfinkel 1973; Pauly 1970). Altruism is neither necessary nor sufficient to justify in-kind transfers, since the altruistic donor might simply be interested in the general well-being (utility) of the beneficiary, in

9 See Weisbrod (1964), Gillespie (1980, 79–80), and Lindsay (1969).
10 This is the familiar argument for providing public goods when exclusion is impossible and true preferences are not revealed. *Supra*, note 9.

which case the traditional argument for cash transfers remains valid.[11] Instead, what is necessary is a plausible explanation of why one group of individuals (potential donors) would want to influence the consumption of particular goods and services by another group of individuals (the potential beneficiaries).

One such explanation is based upon the concept of a 'merit good' (Musgrave 1959; Head 1966, 1969). If donors consider a particular service a 'merit good', they will wish to influence the consumption of that service by another group. An obvious example is child welfare: donors (society, governments) actually wish to correct the preferences of an individual who beats children by compelling him to accept rehabilitative counselling services. Alternatively, donors may hold certain values (right to education, the work ethic) so deeply that they want all individuals exposed to them. This exposure may require provision of in-kind social integration services such as day care, youth centres, summer camps, etc. (see Thurow 1974). Another possibility is that donors wish to ensure that some minimum level of a service is available to all. In this case, donors are concerned with the constrained consumption of social services that low-income individuals experience. Specifically, it is argued that donors derive statisfaction from a reduction in the dispersion of the consumption of services between themselves and low-income earners (Lindsay, 1969).

In general, then, in order to build a case for in-kind provision based on consumption externalities, it is necessary that donors (or governments) have strong convictions about the importance of the benefits flowing from a particular service. If such convictions are present, as they may be for a range of social and rehabilitative services, it is cheaper to work through the price elasticity of demand (consumption subsidies) than through the income elasticity of demand (income subsidies). Further, if the policy is to have recipients increase their consumption of a particular service over that amount implied by their own price and income elasticities and direct cash transfers, then in-kind transfers of some amount of 'basic service' may be justified. Thus, the case against in-kind provision is not as strong as is often suggested.[12] Although one would like to

---

11 A general feeling of 'benevolence' is not enough. It could only lead to 'pareto optimal' redistribution. See Hochman and Rodgers (1969, 1970) for an example of this approach. Criticism is given by Mishan (1972).

12 Again, the relevance of this analysis to the design of intergovernmental grants deserves mention. See Thurow (1966) for an analysis of the design of intergovernmental grants to take advantage of the donee's income and price elasticities of demand. Thurow (1974) also discusses the appropriateness of in-kind transfers when the policy objective is in terms of some basic level of a targeted good. Finally, an interesting paper by McGuire (1973) investigates the interaction between the form of the grant, the objectives of the grantor, and the behavioural response of the local government.

measure the donor's valuation of service consumption by a beneficiary, in practice policy-makers must make subjective judgments about the importance of a particular service to the community.

In addition to deciding whether collective action is appropriate, policy-makers must also choose the form of collective action to take. There are three distinct options: public provision, public funding of voluntary organizations, and subsidized private (profit-making) delivery. Unfortunately, there are no simple criteria to guide this choice. Public provision would ensure coverage, access, and standards. It is therefore necessary for statutory services such as child welfare. Voluntary services foster diversity and experimentation; they often offer innovative programs (which might, however, be politically risky) or cater to sectarian needs. Finally, private provision may be advantageous if the marketplace affects delivery efficiency and service effectiveness. The Canada Assistance Plan acknowledges all three options by extending cost-sharing arrangements to include provincial expenditures on the provision of social services, grants to voluntary agencies, and services purchased on a fee-for-service basis.[13]

There are three particularly important implications of our discussion. First, that social services should be viewed primarily as impure public (mixed) goods, and that the individual consumption component of such collectively consumed goods represents in-kind transfers.[14] Further, in some situations in-kind transfers are preferable to cash transfers, so that there cannot be complete substitution of income security programs for social services delivery. Second, the social services cannot provide an appropriate basis for an anti-poverty strategy, since the primary rationale for government involvement is not the elimination of poverty but the correction of market failures. Third, there is no reason why income redistribution should be linked to service provision, since demand for social services comes from the poor and non-poor alike.

CATEGORIZATION OF SOCIAL SERVICES AND GRADUATED USER CHARGES

The redesign of personal social services implicit in the Social Security Review involved issues 'of somewhat specialized interest to experts in that field', meaning social workers (Ryant 1980, 14). This is hardly surprising, since a great many of the provincial delegates to the Working Party on Social Services 'held MSW

---

13 Bella (1979, 449) argues that the federal government was pressured by the provinces to extend cost-sharing to private agencies.

14 The emphasis must be on mixed goods, since if the service is an indivisible pure public good it cannot exist except as a benefit-in-kind.

degrees' (Kelly 1977, 157); once again, as during the original designing of CAP, the social work profession's influence dominated.[15] The Report of the Working Party on Social Services addressed two issues: the categories of social services that would be eligible for cost-sharing, and the principle of graduated user charges. The working party's report recommended that personal social services be universally accessible to all; it also recommended that services be provided free to those eligible for income assistance, on a subsidized basis to those with incomes just above the level requiring assistance, and at full cost to all others.

The report's categorization of various social services revealed little analytic rigour with respect to the nature or purpose of services; instead it reflected a loose typology based upon target groups and income levels. Initially, five categories were distinguished for the new cost-sharing legislation intended to replace the CAP provisions: services available universally without charge, services to specific groups without charge, services to specific groups with income-tested charges, services to those on assistance without charge, and finally, services 'of a developmental or preventive category for defined communities' (Communiqué, April 30–May 1, 1975, 1–2). Somewhat later, three main classifications of services were proposed: 'services to individuals and families', 'preventive and developmental services for disadvantaged communities', and 'residential services for children and adults' (Communiqué, February 3–4, 1976, 2; reaffirmed in appendix to Communiqué, June 1–2, 1976). Underlying all of the difficulties and ambiguities involved in attempting to categorize personal social services was the firmly held conviction that social services should be provided on a universal basis. The concession to user charges seems to have been almost a fashionable afterthought and an attempt to introduce some 'economic' elements. In any event, Bill C-57 would have permitted cost-sharing for certain services with or without user charges at provincial discretion. However, Bill C-57 also stipulated that user charges must be incorporated in other social services.

Behind the movement to introduce direct charges is the concern that the costs of service provision will rise dramatically as more services become available on a

---

15 The role played by the social work profession in developing social welfare policy in general and the CAP Act in particular must not be underestimated. Almost all the senior officials, including deputy ministers, had an identification with the social work profession (Bella 1977, 1979; Splane 1977). Economists were concerned merely with costs, not program content. However, social workers were outnumbered during the height of the Social Security Review: professional personnel in the Income Security and Social Assistance Program reached 135 on March 31, 1975, up from 55 in September, 1972. As Splane (1977, 221) notes, these were 'almost exclusively persons with academic training deemed relevant to the work undertaken on the quantitative aspects of the Social Security Review'. Most were economists.

universal basis.[16] The issue, then, is whether the increased cost should be borne by the citizen as taxpayer or the citizen as user. The case for imposing a user charge is usually based on three arguments. First, it is argued that a user charge makes costs more explicit to both providers and consumers. This is supposed to lead to greater economy in resource use and a decrease in demand. Demand for social services is therefore assumed to be elastic with respect to price. Second, it is asserted that the price mechanism will encourage market efficiency – in fact, it will do this only if service providers engage in price competition and consumers can judge quality. And third, it is argued that user fees represent a potentially important source of revenue, and thus would permit the expansion of services into new areas.

Carried to its extreme, the argument for direct user charges is equivalent to a call for market provision. But as has already been noted, social service provision has both public and private aspects. Thus a market-pricing system would not guarantee an optimal level of provision or utilization; this is in addition to the usual criticisms involving imperfect competition among suppliers, uninformed consumers, and so forth.

Where society has decided that a particular service must be consumed (i.e., statutory case services such as child welfare), it is difficult to make a case for user charges. Since the choice to consume or not to consume is made by society, public provision without charge is probably the appropriate policy. For example, it seems inappropriate to charge parents for the costs of institutionalizing children they would prefer to have at home.

There are also services for problems which arise as random events. The presence of 'risk' usually brings forth the 'insurance' solution. Under some circumstances, markets for insurance may be absent (Akerlof 1970), and it is argued that 'governments should undertake insurance where the market, for whatever reason, has failed to emerge' (Arrow 1963, 961). If problems arose in a completely random fashion, the optimal insurance program would involve an actuarily based flat-rate premium. Since the insurance premium would be levied on everyone, it would capture the option demand. Again, it is hard to make a case for user charges in addition to the basic premium in a self-financing risk-pooling service. An important requirement for an insurance program to work is that demand for the service be perfectly inelastic with respect to price. For example, events which lead to demand for family counselling may be

16 This is best exemplified by the health care services, which lie outside the scope of this study. See Van Loon (1978) for a discussion of how the effort to control health care costs led to the 'politics' of block funding. Barer, Evans, and Stoddart (1979) provide a complete discussion of the role of user fees in combating the current 'health care cost crisis'.

random, but the demand itself may not be perfectly inelastic. Thus, families might seek counselling only for major problems when the price is high but for minor problems as well when the price falls. Were consumers to behave in this way, some additional price rationing at the point of service might be necessary to guarantee efficient resource allocation and to counter 'moral hazard' (see Pauly, 1968, 531–37 for further discussion). An insurance approach is also inappropriate when the individual has significant control over problems which give rise to demand for services. Again, the argument revolves around the notion of 'moral hazard', only in this case the concern is over excessive take-up.

Until there is some reliable way to separate private and public benefits, there will be no easy rule to tell us if user charges should be levied and, if so, on which services and on what schedule. At present, the best one can do is to judge the relative importance of the private and public benefits of a particular social service. If purely private benefits are thought to be significantly present, a case can be made for user-pay pricing as a means of rationing access to a limited quantity of social services and of reflecting the ability-to-pay principle.[17] Bill C-57 adopted the principle of graduated user fees. However, there are numerous difficulties with this approach. First, the 'price' effect on total demand will not be large – zero price will still be charged to many. Second, a fee schedule uniformly applied to all suppliers does not allow price competition, so market incentives to improve quality will not be present. Third, revenue gains are limited by the costs of collection, and such a collection scheme could be very difficult to implement. Despite these considerable practical difficulties, the major question has to do with access and income distribution. Unless one believes that the distribution of income is perfectly correlated with the distribution of need, the use of graduated-to-income user charges may result in a highly undesirable distribution of access to services.[18] Since the incidence of problems giving rise to a need for social services does not usually respect income class

17 The ability-to-pay principle clearly underlay the graduated user charge design feature. 'Ministers recognized that it is reasonable to expect persons who have financial resources to pay a user charge. ...' (Communiqué, Feb. 3–4, 1976). Again, 'the ability of the user to pay for certain services ... was recognized as an important consideration in setting schedules of user charges (Appendix of Communiqué, June 1–2, 1976, p. 11).

18 For a recent study of user fees and social services, see Krashinsky (1982). This study also proposes an economic theory of in-kind transfers which puts heavy emphasis on the notion of inability, the information costs of measuring inability, and the role of targeting programs and cash transfers. Our views are not much different from Krashinsky's, language aside, and we fully agree that an optimal anti-poverty policy must include both cash transfers and in-kind transfers. However, we tend to place greater emphasis on the notion of social services as a public good.

boundaries, the use of a financial needs or income test to determine access is neither desirable nor appropriate; there is no inherent reason why access to case services should be scaled to income There is a precedent in Canada which might serve as a bench mark: the Hospital Insurance and Diagnostic Services Act. Access to hospital care is determined on the basis of a diagnostic test administered by a professional, but the option to use the service, if need be, is open to all. The rationale for this policy is equally applicable to social services.

7
On poverty, cost-sharing, and Equalization

The previous chapters have examined the Canada Assistance Plan and discussed policy issues associated with the Plan. They have also described various attempts to reform both the delivery designs and the fiscal arrangements of income assistance and social services. This chapter proposes a new basis for cost-sharing under the Canada Assistance Plan.

The final test of any proposal might well be: Is it feasible? Does it make sense under present circumstances? Obviously, the feasibility of the proposal set forth here cannot be gauged in a political or an economic vacuum. The present political climate is notable for its unprecedented degree of uncertainty, with the sharp debate over Equalization and Established Programs Financing adding a harsh colouration to federal-provincial fiscal relations. In the circumstances, any would-be reformer must accept certain political constraints without serious challenge; at the same time, others may as readily be disregarded. For example, the terms of reference for the recent Parliamentary Task Force on Federal-Provincial Fiscal Arrangements specified that its examination of alternatives should 'take place within the context of the government's expenditure plan as set out in the October 18, 1980 budget' (*Fiscal Federalism in Canada* 1981, 1). The restrictions associated with accepting a unilaterally imposed ceiling on federal social spending for designing a new (and permanent?) fiscal arrangement for CAP appear, in our judgment, too severe; consequently our proposal largely ignores them. Besides, as we pointed out in Chapter 3, CAP expenditures are an insignificant fraction of total expenditures on social security. On the other hand, the view that some universal and uniform guaranteed income system, federally financed and federally administered, might be within easy striking distance must be dismissed as being politically unrealistic, even though such a system would be our first choice among possible reforms of the income maintenance system in Canada.

The following section recommends that income assistance and social services be separated and given independent identification. Next, the broad principles of a new cost-sharing formula are outlined. A review of the major analytic assumptions underlying the present study and concluding remarks are given in the final two sections.

SEPARATION OF INCOME ASSISTANCE AND SOCIAL SERVICES

Under current CAP arrangements, income assistance and social services are undifferentiated categories of expenditure eligible for cost-sharing on an identical basis. Yet there would be definite advantages to a cost-sharing formula that treated them separately.

As we have seen, income transfers differ from social services in several important respects. Income maintenance entails redistribution of income – that is, the transfer of rights over private goods. The income benefits transferred are homogeneous units; they can easily be aggregated to determine the total dollar amount involved in any program. What is more important, 'need' and 'basic need' can be defined precisely for the purposes of such programs, and income-testing too can be fairly objective. The adequacy of 'basic support' level may be a matter of dispute, but there is no disputing the object of a specific transfer (namely, a dollar-unit command over private goods and services) or the purpose of the program as a whole (namely, the alleviation of poverty). In contrast, social services comprise a mixture of heterogeneous public goods or in-kind transfers. It would be very difficult to determine a 'basic level' for a standard basket of 'basic services'. Moreover, a potential recipient's 'need' for any particular social service must often be determined through diagnostic testing by professional personnel, and to some extent such testing is necessarily subjective. The object of the transfer may in some cases be difficult to determine, and the goals of the social service itself may not be clear. To summarize, the income assistance programs have a clear objective – the elimination of dire financial hardship – and confining eligibility to those 'in need or likelihood of need' is understandable as a guide. But social services often have little to do with alleviating poverty; consequently CAP's restrictions, which limit access to services to those 'in need', are undesirable.

It is also possible that CAP's failure to distinguish income assistance from social services has retarded program development under one or both headings. Social work professionals have long argued that social services should receive independent standing and not be considered an adjunct to income security policy. Whether according separate identities to income assistance and social services would in fact encourage the independent development of either is impossible to predict; however, separation would undoubtedly result in a new interpretation of such phrases as 'in need or likelihood of need', one that would acknowledge the differences between income assistance and social services.

In 1971, the Croll Committee Report recommended that a sharper distinction be made between income support programs and social services (Canada 1971, Sec. 3, Ch. 1). Bills C-57 and C-55, had either of them received passage when introduced in the late 1970s, would have moved in the direction of establishing an independent status for social services, especially in terms of funding. But the concept of separation had already been anticipated in a 1969 federal report analyzing the respective constitutional roles of the federal and provincial governments with respect to income security and social services (Canada 1969). This report argued that for 'the income redistribution reason' the power to make income payments to persons should be equally shared between Canada and the provinces (p. 66), but that provincial legislatures ought to have exclusive jurisdiction over social services, although Parliament would retain the right to make conditional grants (p. 104).

The federal report argued that an equitable distribution of income across Canada was one of the objectives of Confederation and that disparities in individual incomes were unlikely to be alleviated 'unless Parliament has the power to support the incomes of the poor' (p. 66). However, regional differences in the priority accorded to income redistribution were acknowledged by conceding that 'provinces too must have the power to redistribute income among their residents' (p. 66). The basis of the report's position with respect to social services was the view that local community needs could be more readily met by regional than by national government (p. 96). We concur with this position and now consider how a revised CAP which treats income assistance and social services separately might be cost-shared.

PROPOSAL FOR A NEW COST-SHARING FORMULA

Under the present CAP legislation, Canada shares 50 per cent of the cost of assistance payments paid by the provinces to 'persons in need'. The 'basic allowance' varies from province to province (see Table 7), as does the proportion of the population receiving assistance (see Table 8). Surprisingly, the present cost-sharing formula does not provide for any 'equalization' of the burden of social assistance, making it relatively disadvantageous to precisely those provinces that most need help. We propose that a new cost-sharing formula be established with a standardized basic allowance in mind; that the federal cost-sharing rate (f.c.s.r.) be higher for poorer provinces; that this f.c.s.r. be applied up to some predetermined provincial threshold; and that assistance expenditures by any province beyond this amount be cost-shared at some minimum or base f.c.s.r.

The first step would be the negotiation of a national standard of basic income support, S (this would not preclude adjustments for differences in the cost of living from province to province). The poverty gap of each province can be calculated as $G = q(S - u^*)$, where q is the number of persons with incomes below S and u^* is the mean income of the poor. The poverty gap G establishes for each province a threshold beyond which additional provincial expenditures for assistance would be cost-shared at the base f.c.s.r. – say 50 per cent.[1] For assistance expenditures below G, the federal government would adjust the f.c.s.r. by an index of relative need. We suggest that an appropriate index is the transfer index P(S), calculated for each province.[2] This index rises as the number of poor increases (q), the mean income of the poor falls (u^*), or the mean income of the province falls (u). In other words, the index classifies a province as relatively more needy if it has more poor persons, its poor population is poorer, or its provincial mean income is lower. Because the index P(S) may also be interpreted as the amount each province must 'tax' in order to eliminate poverty in the province, it would also seem appropriate to adjust the f.c.s.r. so that the higher the value of P(S), the larger is the f.c.s.r.[3]

Suppose that the f.c.s.r. varies from a minimum base rate of 50 per cent to some maximum. Why should provincial expenditures for assistance in excess of G be cost-shared at the base f.c.s.r. of 50 per cent rather than continue at each province's P(S)-adjusted f.c.s.r.? The answer lies in the notion of the national standard of basic support. Each province would require the amount G to raise all its residents up to the basic levels. The federal government would acknowledge the provinces' varying abilities to provide this amount by offering a higher

1 The 50 per cent figure for the minimum f.c.s.r. is arbitrary. However tradition might make it difficult to establish a lower minimum cost-sharing rate through federal-provincial negotiation.

2 A poverty index which takes into account the degree of inequality among the poor, such as P_1 and P_2 outlined in Chapter 4, might also be used. P(S) is proposed because of its easy interpretation, although P_1 might be preferable.

3 The principle is more important than the details, which must ultimately result from negotiation. Suppose the base f.c.s.r. is established as 50 per cent; this rate would apply to the province with the lowest P(S) value. Provinces with higher P(S) values would receive a f.c.s.r. higher than 50 per cent by some formula which reflected the extent to which their P(S) value exceeded the smallest P(S) value. A ceiling f.c.s.r. might also be considered. There are endless ways to incorporate the principle.

f.c.s.r. to the poorer provinces. However, certain provinces might choose to exceed the basic level S in their income maintenance programs. Minimum national standards having been met, it seems appropriate that additional expenditures by any particular province would be cost-shared at the minimum base f.c.s.r. uniformly available to all provinces. The advantage of this formula is that it provides for the cost-sharing on an equal basis of a province's 'generosity' and at the same time incorporates an element of 'equalization' for assistance expenditures which fulfil the objective of a national standard. Implicit in the formula, therefore, is the view that a 'basic level of income support' can be defined and that provincial differences in support need not constitute *prima facie* evidence of a lack of national standards. The proposal differs from current provisions in stipulating that a national basic level be legislated into the CAP Act (after negotiation); any variations which might then emerge would truly represent the different degrees to which individual provinces pursued income redistribution and not, as at present, determination by each province of a 'basic allowance'.

The recommended proposal is a conditional cost-sharing formula. Most of the conditions for eligibility under the present cost-sharing formula, such as an absence of residency requirements, would continue to apply. However, the 'need or likelihood of need' provision of the current legislation would be replaced by the income-testing principle – a change that would allow the provinces greater latitude in designing individual programs for specific groups, including the working poor, and enable them to further harmonize their income maintenance policies. Given income-testing as the basis for cost-sharing, both Manitoba's CRISP program and Quebec's supplementation program for the working poor would become cost-sharable.

A similar cost-sharing structure is recommended for social services, with one difference. Because social services are public (or mixed) goods whose heterogeneous nature precludes any operational definition of a 'basic level' of 'basic services', we propose that the national average per capita social service expenditure be used as a standard for the purpose of calculating provincial thresholds. In other words, if x were the national average per capita expenditure on social services, the provincial threshold would simply be x times provincial population. Like social assistance, social services would be cost-shared on a P(s)-adjusted f.c.s.r. basis up to the province's threshold level and at the base f.c.s.r. thereafter. Present eligibility criteria such as the absence of residency requirements would continue to apply.

Implicit in this proposal is the view that it is not possible to determine which services would be included in a 'standard basket' of services, how the cost curve of such a basket would vary by province or scale of effort, etc. Still, the adoption of national average expenditure as the 'standard' expenditure would be more than an exercise in pragmatism. It would be a recognition of the fact that what counts as a social service or when exactly the provision of a social service becomes necessary are matters largely determined by time, place, and circumstance. A province's expenditure for income assistance is a reasonably direct measure of its efforts to reduce poverty, but it cannot be said with the same degree of certainty that a given level of expenditure for social services represents an appropriate contribution to basic national standards. Yet the use of national average expenditure as a standard would still give poorer provinces whose social services expenditures are below the national average the benefit of a more favourable f.c.s.r.

Our recommended reform of the present CAP provisions is firmly in the cost-sharing tradition. It is clearly contrary to the direction of Bill C-55, which would have instituted block funding for the social services. Block funding – that is, the transfer of monies on an unconditional basis – would not be advisable even if the formula for such transfers were adjusted by some index of need such as P(S). Our objection to block funding is simply the familiar one that no guarantee is possible that unconditional transfers will be spent on the intended programs. The CAP legislation derives its rationale from particular objectives, namely income assistance to the poor and the provision of social services. Conditional grants are more appropriate when the aim is to ensure a basic amount of income or services to all individuals. It is also for this reason that we recommend that cost-sharing be calculated separately for income assistance and social services. Income assistance and social services are not proper substitutes: they constitute program responses to distinctly different social welfare objectives.

REVIEW OF MAJOR PREMISES

It is useful at this point to restate the major premises of the study and to set in relief certain interpretative or arguable assumptions. The present study focuses upon the distribution of well-being among individual Canadians; it suggests that past studies of economic federalism have not paid enough attention to this dimension of federalism, that the power to redistribute income must be a shared or concurrent power of the federal and provincial governments, and that the Canada Assistance Plan is the specific creation of a federal structure which assigns responsibility for social policy to one level of government and the major sources of revenue to another. The Canada Assistance Plan is but one of a variety of intergovernmental fiscal techniques which have evolved to solve the 'illogic' of 'co-equally supreme' powers. However, the Canada Assistance Plan is a mechanism designed to achieve specific rather than general objectives. We have identified these specific objectives as the reduction of income poverty and the provision of social services – both of which we have subsumed under the more general heading of social welfare. Income redistribution is viewed as the transfer of individual consumption rights over private goods, while social services are viewed, for the most part, as the provision of public or mixed goods. Although the point has not been treated at length in the present study, we hold that an optimal transfer system would include income transfers as well as transfers of benefits-in-kind.

CONCLUDING REMARKS

This study has examined the Canada Assistance Plan within the broad context of federalism and anti-poverty objectives. Its principal recommendations are that income assistance and social services be accorded separate status, and that a cost-sharing formula be implemented which acknowledges the differences in the burdens placed upon individual provinces by their efforts to combat poverty and provide social services. The proposed cost-sharing arrangement is not meant to preclude the federal government from offering 'special purpose' funds (such as the Rehabilitation Fund of Bill C-55) or 'short term' funds (such as the fund to encourage de-institutionalization recommended by The Parliamentary Task Force Report on Federal-Provincial Fiscal Arrangements 1981, 152) on other terms if it wishes. Nor does the proposal rule out work-activity projects. Since each work-activity project is virtually a unique case, we recommend that no change to the current funding arrangement be made; each approved project from a province should continue to be cost-shared on a 50-50 basis. And since no agreements have ever been signed under the portion of CAP dealing with 'Indian welfare', we have not considered this issue.

The Canada Assistance Plan is overdue for review. CAP has not been the subject of as much controversy and scrutiny as the Established Programs Financing Act or the Equalization formula; this is due in part to the smaller amount of dollars involved in CAP and in part to the fact that there is less dissatisfaction with CAP than with funding arrangements for medical care and education. But the CAP Act deserves no less careful appraisal. At a time when the very constitutional nature of Canada is being realigned, the process of consultation and negotiation over intergovernmental fiscal arrangements should also be open to new thinking.

Appendix A
Federal structure, poverty, and negative taxes

This appendix demonstrates in a more formal fashion certain propositions discussed in Chapter 4, in order to enable the reader to examine in greater detail the nature of the framework and the assumptions.

The important policy questions include: How much should government transfer to those 'in need'? To what extent should 'equalization of incomes' be pursued? What tax rate would be required to finance the chosen level of redistribution? These issues are formalized by specifying a class of indexes based upon the transfer-of-income approach suggested by Kakwani (1977). We first describe the index in terms of anti-poverty objectives.

A common index of poverty or income-need is the head-count ratio

$$F(x^*) = q/N, \qquad\qquad\qquad (A.1)$$

where x^* = some predetermined poverty line,
q = number of individuals with income less than x^*, and
N = total number of individuals in society.

The head-count ratio ignores the degree to which those who are poor fall short of the poverty-income level. An alternative poverty index is the poverty gap, which gives the aggregate dollar amount necessary to eliminate poverty. If u^* is the mean income of those with incomes below x^*, the poverty gap is $q(x^* - u^*)$. However, the poverty gap does not indicate the relative ease or difficulty of eliminating poverty.

The transfer-of-income approach to measuring poverty (Kakwani 1980, ch. 15) proposes the index

$$P(x^*) = \frac{F(x^*)\,(x^* - u^*)}{u} = T(x^*) \qquad (A.2)$$

where u = mean income of society.

The index, $P(x^*)$, is the percentage of total income that must be transferred from the non-poor to the poor in order to raise the income of everyone below the poverty line to x^*. It may also be viewed as the average tax rate, $T(x^*)$, required to finance the elimination of poverty. If $x^* = u$, it can be shown that P leads to the relative mean deviation measure of income inequality (Kakwani 1980, Lemma 5.10, 80); P then becomes the percentage of total income that must be transferred to equalize mean incomes.

Consider a federal state in which the population is divided into k provinces and define

u_i = mean income of province i,
f_i = proportion of national population in province i,
$F_i(x^*)$ = proportion of poor in province i, and
u_i^* = mean income of the poor in province i.

Clearly, we can establish

$$F(x^*) = \Sigma f_i\, F_i(x^*), \text{ and} \qquad (A.3)$$

$$u^* = \frac{1}{F(x^*)}\, \Sigma F_i(x^*)\, u_i^*\, f_i. \qquad (A.4)$$

That is, the proportion of poor in the nation is a weighted average of the proportion of poor in each province, the weights being the population proportion in each province. Similarly, the mean income of the poor in the federation is a weighted average of the mean income of the poor in each province, the weights being proportional to the income share of the poor in each province.

Substituting (A.3) and (A.4) into (A.2) yields

$$T(x^*) = P = 1/u\ \Sigma u_i\, f_i\, P_i, \qquad (A.5)$$

where

$$T_i(x^*) = P_i = \frac{F_i(x^*)(x^* - u_i^*)}{u_i} \tag{A.6}$$

is the transfer index for the ith province. Since $(u_i f_i)/u$ is the income share of province i, (A.5) establishes that: if a population is divided into mutually exclusive provinces, the transfer (poverty) index in the federation is equal to the weighted average of the transfer indexes in each province, the weights being proportional to the income share of each province.

INCOME INEQUALITY AMONG THE POOR

The index $P(x^*)$ ignores income inequality among the poor. To correct this deficiency, some adjustment factor is necessary. Suppose that the Gini index, G^*, is used to measure income inequality among the poor. That is, G^* is restricted to $x \le x^*$. Kakwani (1980, 331) proposes a general class of poverty measures

$$Pg = \frac{F(x^*)}{u}[x^* - u^*g(G^*)] \tag{A.7}$$

where $g(G^*)$ is a monotonic function of G^*, bounded by the closed interval $[0,1]$, $g(0) = 1$, and $g'(G^*) < 0$. This ensures that the poverty index increases with greater inequality among the poor, mean income remaining unchanged. More specifically, if Pg increases with G^* at a constant rate, one suitable poverty index of this general class can be written as

$$P_1 = \frac{F(x^*)}{u}[x^* - u^*(1 - G^*)]. \tag{A.8}$$

This index has the property

$$n_1 = \frac{'G^*}{P_1} \frac{\partial P_1}{\partial G^*} = \frac{u^*G^*}{(x^* - u^*) + u^*G^*} < 1. \tag{A.9}$$

That is, the elasticity of the poverty index with respect to inequality (G^*) is less than unity, implying that if incomes among the poor are redistributed so as to reduce G^* by 1 per cent, the poverty index is reduced by less than 1 per cent. Note that if $x^* = u^*$ then $n_1 = 1$. An alternative poverty index is

$$P_2 = \frac{F(x^*)}{u}[x^* - u^*/(1 + G^*)]. \tag{A.10}$$

Its elasticity with respect to G^* is

$$n_2 = \frac{G^*}{P_2} \frac{\partial P_2}{\partial G^*} = \frac{u^* G^*}{(1 + G^*)(x^* - u^* - x^* G^*)} < 1. \qquad (A.11)$$

It is clear that $n_2 < n_1$, so that P_1 is more sensitive to changes in income inequality among the poor than P_2.

NEGATIVE INCOME TAX AND POVERTY

Income transfer proposals can be analyzed in terms of the components of negative tax plans. A negative tax or guaranteed income plan is characterized by its basic minimum support, S, and its offset taxation rate, B. A 'break-even' level, x^*, can then be defined as that level of income at which transfers or payments cease. For a constant taxation rate, B, the break-even level is equal to S/B. Defining x^* as a 'threshold' level of income, a negative income tax plan operates as follows. Units with incomes exceeding x^* are taxed at a fixed B per cent on the excess; units with incomes below x^* are granted transfer payments (negative taxes), again at a fixed rate of B per cent on the gap between x^* and x. Taxes are, therefore,

$$\begin{aligned} T &= -B\,(x^* - x) \text{ if } x < x^* \\ &= B\,(x - x^*) \text{ if } x > x^* \end{aligned} \qquad (A.12)$$

or simply

$$T = Bx - Bx^*. \qquad (A.13)$$

The disposable income, $d(x)$, of a unit with pre-tax income, x, is

$$\begin{aligned} d(x) &= x - T \\ &= Bx^* + (1-B)x \end{aligned} \qquad (A.14)$$

with mean disposable income

$$u_d = Bx^* + (1-B)\,u^*. \qquad (A.15)$$

The mean disposable income of units below the 'threshold' (breakeven) level, x^*, can be simplified to

$$u^*_d = u^* + B (x^* - u^*). \tag{A.16}$$

Hence, since usually $x^* > u^*$, the mean income of the poor is always raised by negative tax plans. Furthermore, a negative tax plan will result in a more equal distribution of income overall. The Lorenz curve for the entire distribution is shifted towards the egalitarian line; that is, the Lorenz curve for the after-tax income is above the Lorenz curve for the before-tax income (Lorenz Superior). (See Kakwani 1977, 243; 1980, 340 and Theorem 8.2., p. 162 for proofs.)

The Gini index of disposable income, $d(x)$, for $x < x^*$ can be shown to be

$$\tilde{G}^* = \frac{(1-B)\, u^*\, G^*}{u_d^*}, \tag{A.17}$$

and substituting (A.17), (A.16), and (A.15) in the poverty index (A.8) yields the poverty index after imposition of the negative income tax:

$$\tilde{P}_1 = \frac{(1-B)}{u_d}\, F(x^*)\, [x^* - u^* (1-G^*)]. \tag{A.18}$$

This allows calculation of the percentage change in the poverty index,

$$\frac{\tilde{P}_1 - P_1}{P_1} = -\frac{Bx^*}{x^* + (1-B)u}, \tag{A.19}$$

to be expressed as a function of the two key parameters: x^*/u and B (Kakwani 1980, 340). Again, note that if $x^* = u$ – that is, if the breakeven or threshold level is set at the national mean – the percentage reduction in poverty is 100 per cent.

CHOICE OF POVERTY INDEX AND GINI COEFFICIENT

The index P_1 is sensitive to the level of x^*, as well as to the degree of income inequality among those with incomes less than x^*. Intuitively, greater inequality among the poor might imply greater hardship for the extremely poor, and it is desirable in some applications to have the poverty index reflect this. The question is whether the Gini index is appropriate as a measure of income inequality.

Although the Gini coefficient is commonly used, its shortcomings are widely recognized. Other measures of inequality exist, but alternative measures often yield different rankings of income distributions (Atkinson 1970, Sen 1976, Kakwani 1980 and references cited therein). Further, statistical measures of income inequality are frequently proposed without reference to normative notions of social welfare, or else, as in the case of the Gini index, the normative implications may be unacceptable (Atkinson 1970, Das Gupta, Sen and Starrett 1973, and Kakwani 1980, 73–74 for a review). The Gini index is 'indecomposable' (but may be parameterized; see Donaldson and Weymark 1980a, b), or it may show little variation (when Lorenz curves intersect). Worse, when Lorenz curves do intersect, one can always find a social welfare function that will rank the distributions in reverse order to the ranking given by the Gini index (Atkinson 1970). Blackorby and Donaldson (1978, 1980a, 1980b) emphasize that every inequality index implies and is implied by some social welfare function.

Given these indictments against the Gini index, what are the implications of using the Gini index in the present theoretical framework? Within the context of federal-provincial fiscal arrangements, the problem does not arise directly. Fiscal requirements are insensitive to income inequality in the sense that transfer budget totals or average tax rates are unaffected. Two individuals, each $50 below x*, require the same transfer budget as two individuals of whom one is $99 and the other $1 below x*; and in both cases the average tax rate necessary to finance elimination of poverty will be the same. Therefore, the relevant index for fiscal questions is P rather than P_1.

However, the index P_1 is appropriate if one wishes to evaluate income redistribution within a social welfare framework. Within the policy context of negative income tax mechanisms, the post-tax distribution is Lorenz superior to the pre-tax distribution. Consequently, the post-tax distribution is unambiguously more equal than the pre-tax distribution. Further, Atkinson (1970, 247) showed that a ranking of income distributions by the Lorenz criterion is identical to rankings implied by social welfare functions regardless of the form of individual utility functions, provided that Lorenz curves do not intersect. Das Gupta, Sen, and Starrett (1973) and Rothchild and Stiglitz (1973) proved that the social welfare function need only be symmetric and quasi-concave for non-intersecting Lorenz curves to rank distributions in identical fashion to social welfare functions, and Kakwani (1980, Lemma 5.5, Theorem 4.2) showed that the Gini index will rank income distributions in the same order as any symmetric and quasi-concave social welfare function, also provided that Lorenz curves do not intersect.

The Gini index is therefore an appropriate measure of inequality in the present context. The application of a negative income tax does result in non-intersecting Lorenz curves, and given this condition the Gini index is compatible with any social welfare function (that has only mild restrictions) and independent of the form of individual utility functions (as long as these are concave). It is essential to note just what principle is central to the NIT. The basic principle of negative income tax transfer mechanisms is the scaling of benefits in inverse manner to income level.

INCOME TRANSFERS WITH DIFFERENT TAX AND SUBSIDY RATES

The tax rate and the subsidy rate in a negative income tax plan need not be equal. Indeed, equal tax and subsidy rates will not guarantee a purely redistributive result in the sense that post-tax aggregate income will equal pre-tax aggregate income, or $u = u_d$. Pure redistribution requires that total income be kept constant; this requires that the tax rate (B) be different from the subsidy rate (R). Accordingly, disposable income of a unit with pre-tax income x is now given by

$$d(x) = x + R(x^* - x) \text{ if } x < x^*$$
$$= x - B(x - x^*) \text{ if } x > x^* \qquad (A.20)$$

where B and R must satisfy

$$\frac{B}{R} = \frac{P}{(1-x^*/u) + P} . \qquad (A.21)$$

Relation (A.21) is derived assuming $u = u_d$, and P is defined by (A.2). Note that if $R = 1.0$, poverty will be totally eliminated, since any income shortfall will be completely compensated for. Further, $R = 1.0$ implies that this is possible with $B < 1$ only if $x^* < u$. In other words, the only necessary condition for the elimination of poverty is that the poverty level be less than the mean income of society. Finally, if $x^* = u$, note that $B = R$.

The pre- and post-tax poverty indexes incorporating the Gini coefficient can be shown to be related as

$$\tilde{P}_1 = (1 - R) P_1. \qquad (A.22)$$

Therefore, R may be interpreted as the percentage reduction in the poverty index due to the income transfers (Kakwani 1980, 340–41).

ALTERNATIVE DEFINITIONS OF THE TARGET THRESHOLD

The alternative definitions of the target threshold used in the text are

$x^* = $ constant	absolute poverty line
$x^* = au; a < 1$	relative poverty line
$x^* = u$	income egalitarianism
$x^* = S/B; B < 1$	income test and guarantee
$x^* = u + c; c > 0$ or $x^* = $ Max$[u_i]$	equalization

Appendix B
A note on poverty and Equalization

The elimination of poverty or the reduction of income disparities involves redistribution. The fiscal arrangements whereby monies are given to provinces under the 1977 Federal-Provincial Fiscal Arrangements and Established Programs Financing Act also involve redistribution in a sense. Another arrangement is the practice whereby Canada gives monies to the provinces on a formula basis so that 'all provinces are able to provide reasonably comparable levels of public services without resorting to unduly burdensome levels of taxation' (Federal-Provincial Tax Structure Committee 1966, 15). These federal-provincial transfers are referred to as Equalization payments or Equalization grants.

This note employs our general theoretical framework to detail a relationship between equalization of income for individuals and Equalization transfers to the provinces. We suggest how a needs-adjusted amendment to the existing Equalization scheme could provide a partial synthesis of social welfare and fiscal finance concerns.

THE FORMULA FOR EQUALIZATION

Equalization ensures that each province has access to revenues equivalent to that amount obtained from applying national average tax rates to national average tax bases. Equalization may be represented algebraically by the formula

$$E = TR \left[\frac{Pp}{Pc} - \frac{Bp}{Bc} \right], \tag{B.1}$$

where E is the Equalization payment to a province, Pp is provincial population, Pc is the total population of Canada, Bp and Bc are respectively the provincial and Canadian tax bases, and TR is total tax revenue. The bracketed expression represents 'fiscal deficiency' if positive and 'fiscal excess' if negative. A province receives Equalization transfers if its ratio of total population exceeds its share of the tax base.[1] Consequently, Equalization can achieve some degree of fiscal uniformity where tax and spending powers are constitutionally divided between levels of governments.[2] Although provinces with a fiscal deficiency receive Equalization payments, provinces with a fiscal excess are not 'taxed' on their excess. Hence the formula is assymetric and non-redistributive in the interprovincial sense, since rich provinces neither transfer resources to 'have not' provinces nor contribute directly to the pool of funds for such transfers.

1 Description of the formula draws on Courchene and Beavis (1973). The notation has been simplified for convenience.
2 The technical mechanics of Equalization are tangential to our main purpose but are nevertheless interesting. For example, the present Equalization formula equalizes revenue with the implicit assumption of equal costs or at least a balancing-out of differences in costs of an array of services (Courchene and Copplestone 1980, 48). Further, recent changes in the cost-sharing aspect of established programs have essentially converted these grants to unconditional status, with figures to be escalated by the annual rate of growth in per capita gross national product (Courchene 1979, 12). These features may be analyzed in terms of the theory of exact index numbers. Suppose we have the Laspeyres index measure of revenue change or cost change,

$$L = \frac{\Sigma t^1 B^0}{\Sigma t^0 B^0},$$

where B^0 is tax or cost base in the initial year, and t^1 and t^0 are tax rates or costs in later and initial years respectively. Consider a 'tax rate' or 'cost change'. If each province has its own index of revenue change.

$$L^i \quad \frac{\Sigma t^1 B_i}{\Sigma t^0 B_i}, \text{ where } i = a, b$$

the national index (for a country with two provinces) can be written as

$$L = \frac{\Sigma t^1 B}{\Sigma t^0 B} = \frac{\Sigma t^1 Ba}{\Sigma t^0 Ba} \frac{\Sigma t^0 Ba}{\Sigma t^0 (Ba + Bb)} + \frac{\Sigma t^1 Bb}{\Sigma t^0 Bb} \frac{\Sigma t^0 Bb}{\Sigma t^0 (Ba + Bb)}$$

$$= L^a (Ya / Y) + L^b (Yb / Y).$$

which is a weighted sum of provincial Laspeyres indexes, the weights being each province's share of total national revenue. In terms of the theory of true 'cost indexes', the Laspeyres index is greater than or equal to the 'ture' index (Phlips 1974, Ch. 5). This example illustrates how the detailed mechanics of Equalization or unconditional grants might be analyzed using other than a fiscal finance approach. To our knowledge, this has never been done and represents, perhaps, a useful avenue for further research.

A fundamental assumption by most writers is that Equalization is a matter between levels of government and is related only indirectly, if at all, to individual citizens (e.g., Graham 1980). Under this view, appeal is made to the principle of fiscal equity whereby 'similarly situated citizens in different provinces are to receive comparable public services and bear comparable tax burdens'. Additionally, Equalization is 'justified and necessary only with respect to public goods' (*Ibid.*, 45, 46). Therefore schemes to 'equalize' individual incomes through, say, a negative income tax are not a substitute for Equalization grants to have-not provinces (*Ibid.*, 47; see also Usher 1980a, 27).

Another source of contention is the question of whether the purpose of Equalization is to ensure for every Canadian, regardless of his province of domicile, some level of 'basic services', or whether it is to ensure for him the level of 'average services' in Canada. Courchene and Copplestone (1980, 23) see the lack of definition of basic services as a serious flaw. For others (Graham 1980, 48–49), the issue of defining basic services does not arise because the average overall cost is taken as the 'standard expenditure' on which Equalization is based.

From our perspective, the predominant issue respecting Equalization is the extent of redistribution. The assymmetric feature of the Equalization formula implies that Equalization is neither self-financing nor redistributive. The fact that it is not redistributive on an interprovincial basis is independent of whether some fixed level of 'basic services' or the 'average level' collectively determined by all provinces is employed for calculation purposes, since fiscal deficiencies are removed by intergovernmental transfers from the federal government. Hence, the present arrangement is merely 'compensatory', in the sense that lower-revenue provinces receive grants from the central government to raise their total resources to some predetermined target level; it is not redistributive across provinces. Removal of the assymmetric feature of Equalization would enhance inter-provincial redistribution. Simultaneously, definition of a target threshold of basic services below the national average level would result in partial revenue equalization. Establishing the target threshold as the national average would imply full revenue equalization, but setting it in excess of the national average, even with a symmetric Equalization formula, would require compensatory transfers in addition to redistributive transfers. A provincial revenue-sharing pool alone would not be sufficient, since an externally defined level of 'basic services' (say, that level enjoyed by the two richest provinces) would mean an overall net fiscal deficiency in the system. Given a provincial revenue-sharing arrangement and an externally defined target threshold in excess of the national average, additional revenues would have to be forthcoming. In a federal system with shared tax and spending powers, the level of government with excess fiscal capacity has the greater power to shoulder the responsibility for Equalization. In Canada, it has generally been the national government that possesses the excess fiscal capacity.

NEEDS-ADJUSTED EQUALIZATION AND NATIONAL POVERTY

There have been many proposals for the reform of Equalization. Davenport (1979) suggests that the 'have' provinces be taxed for Equalization transfers to the 'have not' provinces on the basis of an Adjusted Personal Income (API) measure. His scheme would remove the assymetric feature of the formula and redefine the tax base. Courchene (1979, 1980) has proposed a two-tiered system. The first tier, like the present Equalization scheme, would be financed federally. The second tier would be a provincially financed, purely redistributive plan of the negative income tax type – in effect, a 'fully equalizing' revenue-sharing pool. Other possibilities include adjusting Equalization transfers for relative incomes and the size of the urbanized population (Boadway 1980, 72 and Courchene and Copplestone 1980), or incorporating some consideration of fiscal need (Clark 1969).

We indicate how the poverty index, P, might be incorporated in an Equalization formula. The present Equalization formula is given by

$$E = TR\left[\frac{N_i}{N} - \frac{B_i}{B_c}\right], \tag{B.1}$$

where the subscripts c and i refer respectively to Canada and a given province. Since the poverty measure

$$P = T(x^*) = \frac{F(x^*)(x^* - u^*)}{u} \tag{A.2}$$

can be interpreted as an 'average tax rate', application of (A.5) and (A.6) yields

$$P{\cdot}u = \Sigma f_i u_i P_i \tag{B.2}$$

$$P{\cdot}u{\cdot}N = \Sigma N_i u_i P_i, \text{ or}$$

$$t_c B_c = \Sigma \frac{N_i}{N} t_c B_c = \sum_i t_i B_i$$

where $P = t_c$, $P_i = t_i$, $f_i = N_i / N$, $B_c = uN$, and $B_i = u_i N_i$, N_i is the population of province i, and N is the total population.

Fixing x^*, equalization for any province can be written as

$$E = \frac{N_i}{N} t_c B_c - t_i B_i \qquad \text{(B.3)}$$

Manipulating (B.3) and denoting $t_c B_c$ as TR yields

$$E = TR \left[\frac{N_i}{N_c} - \left(\frac{t_i}{t_c} \right) \frac{B_i}{B_c} \right] \qquad \text{(B.4)}$$

which is formula (B.1) with an adjustment factor.

Since $t_i = P_i$, $B_i = u_i N_i$, $t_c = P$ and $B_c = uN$, it is clear that (B.4) represents a 'needs-adjusted' equalization formula. Recall that

$$t_i = P_i = \frac{F_i (x^*)(x^* - u_i^*)}{u_i} \qquad \text{(A.6)}$$

and we have

$$\frac{t_i}{t_c} = \frac{P_i}{P} = \frac{F_i(x^*)(x^* - u_i^*)u}{F(x^*)(x^* - u^*) u_i} \qquad \text{(B.5)}$$

Accordingly, the adjustments for relative need take into account the relative amount of poverty in a given province or, equivalently, the relative provincial tax effort required to eliminate poverty in that province (since the measure P can also be interpreted as an average tax rate).

CONCLUSION

Equalization formula (B.5) has the following significant implications. First and most important, it incorporates the concept of relative need. The particular index of need used, namely the transfer index $P = T(x^*)$, ensures that each province receives the appropriate intergovernmental transfer to combat poverty or redistribute individual incomes. Although Equalization may continue to be viewed as a matter of grants between governments, formula (B.5) means that any nationally specified anti-poverty objective or desired degree of individual redistribution can be made consistent with a system of formula intergovernmental grants.

Since P is a poverty measure, the normative basis for adjusting the Equalization formula by this index has great intuitive appeal. The index P can also be interpreted as the average tax rate necessary to eliminate provincial poverty, since it relates the extent of poverty in a given province to its average income level. Consequently, an element of 'tax capacity' is incorporated, albeit the notion of tax capacity refers only to anti-poverty effort. This suggests that Equalization grants cannot be equitably replaced by abatements of equal tax points to all provinces.

The formula (B.5) leaves open the definition of the target threshold x^* and the question of whether Equalization should constitute mere revenue-pooling or possibly include net transfers between levels of government. The target threshold x^* could be set either at some 'basic level' so that $x^* < u$, or set at the national average level so that $x^* = u$. Or $x^* + c > u$, in which case net funds would be necessary.

Equalization is fundamentally a system of unconditional transfers. Whether or not richer provinces should contribute directly to Equalization and thereby make it redistributive in an interprovincial sense is a matter for debate. So too is the question of federal compensatory transfers to provinces to bring individual provincial revenues up to some arbitrary level. But that the amount of unconditional transfers should vary according to provincial need is a view of long standing. It may even be traced back to the Statutory Subsidies and the various 'debt adjustment' or 'special need' grants at Confederation. In 1927, the Duncan Commission introduced additional interim grants for the Atlantic Provinces, and the Depression saw special grants to the Prairies. More recently, the Atlantic Provinces Adjustment Grants (initiated in 1958 and called 'Additional Grants' since 1961) have in effect provided unconditional assistance to provinces deemed in need (Moore, Perry, and Beach 1966, 2, 8, 11, 13, 61, 76). In one form or another, then, there have long been federal transfers to the provinces that implicitly recognize the factor of relative need. The originality of proposing a poverty index for the Equalization formula is to clarify the importance and implications of the target threshold, x^*, and to demonstrate that there need not be a conflict between fighting poverty or equalizing individual incomes and the notion of Equalization grants as purely inter-governmental transfers. It is possible, therefore, to reconcile a fiscal finance approach with a social welfare view of social policy in a federal state.

Appendix C
Income inequality across provinces, sensitivity and rankings by Atkinson's measure

Statistical summary measures of income inequality cannot avoid introducing distributional values. In fact, Blackorby and Donaldson (1978, 1980a, b) have recently demonstrated that every index of inequality implies, and is implied by, some social welfare function. The social welfare function, in this context, simply specifies explicitly the weight society attaches to inequality in the distribution. One particular class of social welfare functions (symmetric, additively separable) leads to the Atkinson measure of income inequality:

$$I = 1 - [\Sigma_i (y_i/u)^{1-\epsilon} \ f(y_i)]^{1/1-\epsilon} ,$$

where y_i denotes the income of those in the ith range, u is mean income, and $f(\cdot)$ represents the proportion of the population with incomes in the ith range (Atkinson 1970). The measure $1 - I$ is naturally interpreted as the proportion of present total income that would be required to achieve the present level of social welfare if income were distributed equally. For example, a value of $I = .20$ means that society could maintain the present level of social welfare with 80 per cent of present total income if income were distributed equally. The index I contains a parameter, ϵ, which indicates the relative sensitivity of I to transfers at different levels of income. As ϵ becomes very large, more weight is given to transfers at the lower end of the distribution; as ϵ approaches zero, distributions are ranked solely according to total income. The parameter ϵ is a measure of the degree of inequality-aversion (Atkinson 1970, 257), and the inequality index I is a measure of the potential gains from redistribution (Atkinson 1975, 49). It is interesting to calculate for the different provinces of Canada the inequality measure I and see how the inequality measures for provinces alter rankings for different values of the inequality-aversion parameter. It is essential, however, to

Figure A.1
Sensitivity of I to variations in ∈

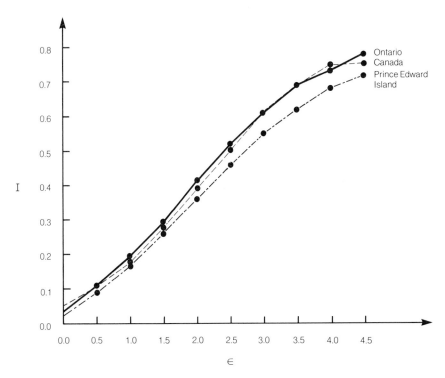

emphasize that the Atkinson measure is based upon special assumptions concerning the social welfare function.

Figure A.1 displays the sensitivity of the measure I to variations in the parameter ε. The measure I is plotted for Canada and for the provinces with the highest mean income (Ontario) and lowest mean income (Prince Edward Island). Since it is apparent that these curves cross, the ranking of provinces by I will change for different values of the parameter ε.

Figure A.2 illustrates the sensitivity of provincial rankings according to I for various values of ε. For example, Newfoundland has the highest value for I at ε = 0.0 and the lowest value for I at ε = 2.5.

Figure A.2
Ranking of income distributions for different values of ∈

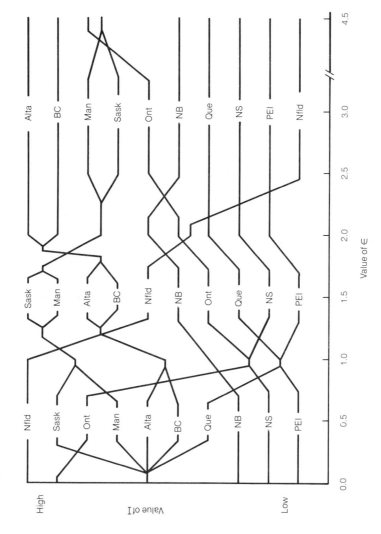

Bibliography

Aaron, H. and M. McGuire (1970) 'Public Goods and Income Distribution' *Econometrica* 38, 907–20

Aaron, H. and G. Von Furstenberg (1971) 'The Inefficiency of Transfers in Kind: The Case of Housing Allowance' *Western Economic Journal* 9, 184–91

Akerlof, G. (1970) 'The Market for Lemons: Qualitative Uncertainty and the Market Mechanism' *Quarterly Journal of Economics* 84, 488–500

Akerlof, G. (1978) 'The Economics of "Tagging" as Applied to the Optimal Income Tax, Welfare Programs, and Manpower Planning' *American Economic Review* 68, 8–19

Armitage, A. (1979) *Social Welfare in Canada* (Toronto: McClelland and Stewart Limited)

Arrow, K. (1963) 'Uncertainty and the Welfare Economics of Medical Care' *American Economic Review* 53, 941–73

Atkinson, A.B. (1970) 'On the Measurement of Inequality' *Journal of Economic Theory* 2, 244–63

Atkinson, A. (1975) *The Economics of Inequality* (Oxford: Clarendon Press)

Barer, M., R. Evans and G. Stoddart (1979) *Controlling Health Care Costs by Direct Charges to Patients: Snare or Delusion?* (Toronto: Ontario Economic Council)

Bella, L. (1977) 'The Canada Assistance Plan' *The Social Worker* 45, 86–92

Bella, L. (1979) 'The Provincial Role in the Canadian Welfare State: the Influence of Provincial Social Policy Initiatives on the Design of the Canada Assistance Plan' *Canadian Public Administration* 22, 439–52

Bishop, J. (1977) 'Jobs, Cash Transfers, and Marital Instability: A Review of the Evidence' (Madison: Institute for Research on Poverty, University of Wisconsin)

Blackorby, C. and D. Donaldson (1978) 'Measures of Relative Equality and Their Meaning in Terms of Social Welfare' *Journal of Economic Theory* 18, 59–80

Blackorby, C. and D. Donaldson (1980a) 'A Theoretical Treatment of Indices of Absolute Inequality' *International Economic Review* 21, 107–36

Blackorby, C. and D. Donaldson (1980b) 'Ethical Indices for the Measurement of Poverty' *Econometrica* 48, 1053–60

Boadway, R. (1980) *Intergovernmental Transfers in Canada* (Toronto: The Canadian Tax Foundation)

Boadway, R.W. and H.M. Kitchen (1980) *Canadian Tax Policy* (Toronto: The Canadian Tax Foundation)

Breton, A. (1965) 'A Theory of Government Grants' *Canadian Journal of Economics and Political Science* 31, 175–87

Breton, A. (1966) 'Public Goods (and Federalism): A Reply' *Canadian Journal of Economics and Political Science* 32, 238–42

Breton, A. and A. Scott (1978) *The Economic Constitution of Federal States* (Toronto: University of Toronto Press)

Bryden, K. (1974) *Old Age Pensions and Policy-Making in Canada* (Montreal: McGill-Queen's University Press)

Canada (1969) *Income Security and Social Services* Working Paper on the Constitution (Ottawa: Queen's Printer).

Canada. Dept. of Finance (1981) *Economic Review* (Ottawa: Supply and Services)

Canada. National Health and Welfare, *Canada Assistance Plan Annual Reports (1967–1979)* (Ottawa: Supply and Services)

Canada, National Health and Welfare (1970) *Income Security for Canadians* (Ottawa: Queen's Printer)

Canada, National Health and Welfare (1973) *Working Paper on Social Security in Canada* (Ottawa) (the Orange Paper)

Canada, National Health and Welfare (1973) *Working Paper on Social Security in Canada* (Ottawa) (the Orange Paper)

Canada. National Health and Welfare (1978) 'Summary of the Principal Components of the Social Services Financing Bill', 'The Federal Legislation on Financing Social Services – 1978' and 'News Release, May 12, 1978' (Ottawa: Supply and Services)

Canada. National Health and Welfare (1979) *Social Security Statistics: Canada and Provinces 1950–51, 1977–78*, (Ottawa: Supply and Services)

Canada. Special Senate Committee on Poverty (1971) *Report: Poverty in Canada*

Canada. Parliament. Task Force on Federal-Provincial Fiscal Arrangements (1981) *Fiscal Federalism in Canada* (Ottawa: Supply and Services)

Canadian Council on Social Development (1979) *Canadian Fact Book on Poverty 1979* (Ottawa: CCSD)

Canadian Intergovernmental Conference Secretariat (1980) *The Income Security System in Canada: A Report prepared by The Interprovincial Task Force on Social Security for the Interprovincial Conference of Ministers Responsible for Social Services* (Ottawa)

Canadian Tax Foundation (1981) *The National Finances: An Analysis of the Revenues and Expenditures of the Government of Canada 1980–81* (Toronto: Canadian Tax Foundation)

Clark, D.H. (1969) *Fiscal Need and Revenue Equalization Grants* (Toronto: Canadian Tax Foundation)

Courchene, T.J. (1979) *Refinancing the Canadian Federation: A Survey of the 1977 Fiscal Arrangements Act* (Montreal: C.D. Howe Research Institute)

Courchene, T.J. (1980) 'Energy and Equalization' in *Energy Policies for the 1980s: An Economic Analysis, Volume 1* (Toronto: Ontario Economic Council)

Courchene, T.J. and D.A. Beavis (1973) 'Federal-Provincial Tax Equalization: An Evaluation' *Canadian Journal of Economics* 6, 483–502

Courchene, T.J. and G.H. Copplestone (1980) 'Alternative Equalization Programs: Two-Tier Systems' in Richard M. Bird, ed. *Fiscal Dimensions of Canadian Federalism* (Toronto: Canadian Tax Foundation)

Das Gupta, P., A.K. Sen, and D. Starrett (1973) 'Notes on the Measurement of Inequality' *Journal of Economic Theory* 6, 180–87

Davenport, P. (1979) 'Equalization Payments and Regional Disparities', Paper presented at the annual meeting of The Canadian Economics Association, Saskatoon.

Donaldson, D. and J. Weymark (1980a) 'A Single-Parameter Generalization of the Gini Indices of Inequality' *Journal of Economic Theory* 22, 67–86

Donaldson, D. and J. Weymark (1980b) 'Ethically Flexible Gini Indices for Income Distributions in the Continuum' unpublished manuscript

Doyle, R. (1978) 'Canada's Social Security Review' *Australian Journal of Social Issues* 13, 26–39

Dyck, R. (1976) 'The Canada Assistance Plan: The Ultimate in Co-operative Federalism' *Canadian Public Administration* 19, 587–602

Federal-Provincial Tax Structure Committee (1966) *Proceedings of the Federal-Provincial Tax Structure Committee* (Ottawa: Queen's Printer)

Garfinkel, I. (1973) 'Is In-kind Redistribution Efficient', *Quarterly Journal of Economics* 87, 320–30

Gillespie, W. Irwin (1980) *The Redistribution of Income in Canada* (Ottawa: Gage Publishing Limited)

Graham, J. (1980) 'Comment' in R. Bird, ed. *Fiscal Dimensions of Canadian Federalism* (Toronto: Canadian Tax Foundation)

Guest, D. (1980) *The Emergence of Social Security in Canada* (Vancouver: University of British Columbia Press)

Head, J.G. (1966) 'On Merit Goods' *Finanzarchiv* 26, 4–10

Head, J.G. (1969) 'Merit Wants Revisited' *Finanzarchiv* 28, 214–25

Heagle, D.G. (1978) 'Crisis in Cost Sharing – What is Going On?' in *Canadian Conference on Social Development, 1978, Proceedings* (Ottawa: The Canadian Council on Social Development)

Hepworth, H.P. (1975) *Personal Social Services in Canada: A Review* (Ottawa: Canadian Council on Social Development) Eleven Volumes

Hochman, H.M. and J.D. Rodgers (1969) 'Pareto Optimal Redistribution' *American Economic Review* 59, 542–57

Hochman, H.M. and J.D. Rogers (1970) 'Pareto Optimal Redistribution: A Reply' *American Economic Review* 60, 997–1002

Hum, D. (1980a) 'Poverty, Policy and Social Experimentation in Canada: Background and Chronology' in *Reflections on Canadian Incomes* (Ottawa: Economic Council of Canada)

Hum, D. (1980b) 'Negative Income Tax Experiments: A Descriptive Survey with Special Reference to Work Incentives' in *Reflections on Canadian Incomes* (Ottawa: Economic Council of Canada) 127–47

Hum, D. (1981a) *Unemployment Insurance and Work Effort: Issues, Evidence and Policy Directions* (Toronto: Ontario Economic Council)

Hum, D. (1981b) 'Canada's Administrative Experience with Negative Income Taxation' *Canadian Taxation* 3, 2–16

Hum, D. and H. Stevens (1980) 'The Manitoba White Paper on Tax Credit Reform: A Critique' *Canadian Taxation* 2, 129–34

Johnson, A.W. (1975) 'Canada's Social Security Review (1973–75): The Central Issues' *Canadian Public Policy – Analyse de Politiques* 1, 456–72

Kahn, A.J. (1979) *Social Policy and Social Services, Second Edition* (New York: Random House, Inc.)

Kakwani, N. (1977) 'Measurement of Poverty and Negative-Income Tax' *Australian Economic Papers* 17, 237–48

Kakwani, N. (1980) *Income Inequality and Poverty* (Washington: Oxford University Press for the World Bank)

Kelly, M. (1977) 'The New Social Services Legislation – What Next?' *The Social Worker* 45, 156–60

Kesselman, J. (1969) 'Labor-Supply Effects of Income, Income-Work, and Wage Subsidies' *Journal of Human Resources* 4, 275–92

Kesselman, J. (1973) 'A Comprehensive Approach to Income Maintenance: SWIFT' *Journal of Public Economics* 2, 59–88

Kesselman, J. and I. Garfinkel (1978) 'Professor Friedman, meet Lady Rhys-Williams: NIT vs. CIT' *Journal of Public Economics* 10, 179–216

Krashinsky, M. (1977) *Day Care and Public Policy in Ontario* (Toronto: Ontario Economic Council)

Krashinsky, M. (1981) *User Charges in the Social Services: an Economic Theory of Need and Inability* (Toronto: Ontario Economic Council)

Lindsay, C.M. (1969) 'Medical Care and the Economics of Sharing' *Economica* 36, 351–62

Mallory, J.R. (1965) 'The Five Faces of Federalism' in Crepeau, P.A. and C.B. MacPherson (eds), *The Future of Canadian Federalism* (Toronto: University of Toronto Press) 3–15

Marshall, T.H. (1955) *Social Policy* (London: Hutchinson University Library)

May, R.J. (1969) *Federalism and Fiscal Adjustment* (London: Oxford Clarendon Press)

McGuire, M. (1973) 'Notes on Grants-in-Aid and Economic Interactions among Governments' *Canadian Journal of Economics* 6, 207–221

McLure, C.E. (1968) 'Merit Wants: A Normatively Empty Box' *Finanzarchiv* 27, 474–83

Mishan, E.J. (1972) 'The Futility of Pareto-Efficient Distributions' *American Economic Review* 62, 971–76

Moore, A.M., J. Harvey Perry and Donald I. Beach (1966) *The Financing of Canadian Federation* (Toronto: Canadian Tax Foundation)

Musgrave, R.A. (1959) *The Theory of Public Finance* (New York: McGraw-Hill Book Co. Inc.)

National Council of Welfare (1981) *The Working Poor: People and Programs* (Ottawa: NCW)

Norquay, G. (1979) 'Death-Knell Sounded for Improved Social Services Funding Scheme' *Perception* 2, 36–37

Oates, W.E. (1968) 'The Theory of Public Finance in a Federal System' *Canadian Journal of Economics* 1, 45–48

Oates, W.E. (1972) *Fiscal Federalism* (New York: Harcourt Brace Jovanovich)

Orr, L.L. (1976) 'Income Transfers as a Public Good: An Application to AFDC' *American Economic Review* 66, 359–71

Pauly, M. (1968) 'The Economics of Moral Hazard: Comment' *American Economic Review* 63, 531–37

Pauly, M. (1970) 'Efficiency in the Provision of Consumption Subsidies' *Kyklos* 23, 33–57

Phlips, L. (1974) *Applied Consumption Analysis* (New York: American Elsevier Publishing Co., Inc.)

Quebec. Royal Commission of Inquiry on Health and Social Welfare (1971) *Report* (Government of Quebec)

Riches, G. (1977) 'Which Way for Personal Social Services in Canada, Now?' *The Social Worker* 45, 185–91

Riches, G. (1978) 'FIP Flops' *Perception* 1, 42

Ross, D.P. (1981) *The Working Poor: Wage Earners and the Failure of Income Security Policies* (Toronto: James Lorimer and Canadian Institute for Economic Policy)

Rothchild, M. and J.E. Stiglitz (1973) 'Some Further Results on the Measurement of Inequality' *Journal of Economic Theory* 6, 188–204

Russell, P. (1965) *Leading Constitutional Decisions*, rev. ed. (Toronto: McClelland and Stewart)

Ryant, J. (1980) 'Federal Provincial Consultation in Social Policy Formulation: A Canadian Example' unpublished manuscript

Safarian, A.E. (1974) *Canadian Federalism and Economic Integration*, Constitutional Study prepared for the Government of Canada (Ottawa: Information Canada)

Safarian, A.E. (1980) *Ten Markets or One? Regional Barriers to Economic Activity in Canada* (Toronto: Ontario Economic Council)

Saskatchewan, Department of Social Services (1976) *Income Support and Supplementation: The Saskatchewan Experience with FIP and SAP*

Saskatchewan Information Services (1976) 'Criticism of FIP Misleading' Press Release dated Nov. 8, 1976

Scott, A.D. (1964) 'The Economic Goals of Federal Finance' *Public Finance* 19, 241–88

Sen, A. (1976) 'Poverty: An Ordinal Approach to Measurement' *Econometrica* 44, 219–32

Simeon, R. (1972) *Federal-Provincial Diplomacy* (Toronto: University of Toronto Press)

Simpson, W. (1981) 'The Relationship Between Wages and Family Income in Canada', Discussion Paper (Ottawa: Labour Canada)

Smiley, D. (1963) *The Rowell-Sirois Report, Book 1* (Toronto: McClelland and Stewart, Carleton Library)

Splane, R. (1977) 'Social Policy-Making in the Government of Canada: Reflections of a Reformist Bureaucrat' in S. Yelaga (ed) *Canadian Social Policy* (Waterloo: Wilfrid Laurier Press) 209–26

Statistics Canada (1978) *Canada Year Book 1978–1979* (Ottawa: Supply and Services)

Statistics Canada (1978) *Social Security, National Programs 1978*, Cat. No. 86–201 (Annual) (Ottawa).

Tamagno, E. (1979) 'The Quebec Income Supplementation Plan' *Canadian Taxation* 1, 63–66

Thurow, L.C. (1966) 'The Theory of Grants-in-Aid' *National Tax Journal* 19, 373–77

Thurow, L.C. (1971) 'The Income Distribution as a Pure Public Good' *Quarterly Journal of Economics* 75, 327–36

Thurow, L.C. (1974) 'Cash Versus In-Kind Transfers' *American Economic Review* (Proceedings) 64, 190–95

Usher, D. (1978) 'The English Response to the Prospect of the Separation of Quebec' *Canadian Public Policy – Analyse de Politiques* 4, 57–70

Usher, D. (1980a) 'How Should the Redistributive Power of the State be Divided between Federal and Provincial Governments?' *Canadian Public Policy – Analyse de Politiques* 6, 16–29

Usher, D. (1980b) 'A Reply' *Canadian Public Policy – Analyse de Politiques* 6, 667–69

Van Loon, R. (1978) 'From Shared Cost to Block Funding and Beyond: The Politics of Health Insurance in Canada' *Journal of Health Politics, Policy and Law* 2, 454–78

Van Loon, R. (1979) 'Reforming Welfare in Canada' *Public Policy* 27, 469–504

Wallace, E. (1950) 'The Origin of the Social Welfare State in Canada, 1867–1900' *Canadian Journal of Economics and Political Science* 16, 383–93

Weisbrod, B.A. (1964) 'Collective-Consumption Services of Individual-Consumption Goods' *Quarterly Journal of Economics* 78, 471–77

Weldon, J.C. (1966) 'Public Goods (and Federalism)' *Canadian Journal of Economics and Political Science* 32, 230–38

West, E.G. and M. McKee (1980) *Minimum Wages: The New Issues in Theory, Evidence, Policy and Politics* (Ottawa: Supply and Services Canada)

West, E.G. and S.L. Winer (1980a) 'The Individual, Political Tension and Canada's Quest for a New Constitution' *Canadian Public Policy – Analyse de Politiques* 6, 1–15

West, E.G. and S.L. Winer (1980b) 'Will Federal Centralization Help the Poor?' *Canadian Public Policy—Analyse de Politiques* 6, 662–67

Wheare, K.C. (1963) *Federal Government* 4th ed. (London: Oxford University Press)